Revitalizing Western Economies

A New Agenda
for Business
and Government

Russell L. Ackoff

Paul Broholm

Roberta Snow

Revitalizing Western Economies

Jossey-Bass Publishers

San Francisco • Washington • London • 1984

REVITALIZING WESTERN ECONOMIES
A New Agenda for Business and Government
by Russell L. Ackoff, Paul Broholm, and Roberta Snow

Copyright © 1984 by: Jossey-Bass Inc., Publishers
433 California Street
San Francisco, California 94104
&
Jossey-Bass Limited
28 Banner Street
London EC1Y 8QE

Library of Congress Cataloging in Publication Data

Ackoff, Russell Lincoln (date)
    Revitalizing western economies.

    (Jossey-Bass management series) (Jossey-Bass social
and behavioral science series)
    Bibliography: p. 191
    Includes index.
    1. Economic history—1945-   . 2. Unemployment.
3. Industry and state. 4. Industrial management.
5. Service industries. I. Broholm, Paul, 1955-
II. Snow, Roberta, 1955-   . III. Title. IV. Series.
V. Series: Jossey-Bass social and behavioral science
series.
HC59.A674   1984   330'.09   84-47977
ISBN 0-87589-609-X

Manufactured in the United States of America

The paper in this book meets the guidelines for
permanence and durability of the Committee on
Production Guidelines for Book Longevity of the
Council on Library Resources.

JACKET DESIGN BY WILLI BAUM

FIRST EDITION

Code 8432

A joint publication in
The Jossey-Bass Management Series
and
The Jossey-Bass Social and Behavioral Science Series

Foreword

I should state at the outset that I have a strong bias when it comes to the works of Russell L. Ackoff and his colleagues. I find that one work of theirs is generally equal to the works of a hundred others in stimulating my thoughts and my passions. This latest example is no exception.

Russell Ackoff is, of course, one of the most provocative thinkers in the social sciences. He is without doubt one of the most eminent practitioners of the systems approach writing today. He and his colleagues possess the uncanny ability to cut to the core of a complex problem more quickly, more directly, and more simply than any social analysts or critics of whom I am aware.

In the present volume, Ackoff and his colleagues analyze one of the most vexing problems facing Western democracies today: the horrible shape of their economies and traditional industries. The authors analyze and discard conventional solutions

to the problem and conclude that nothing less than a radical restructuring of the *operations* of government will suffice to get
out of our current economic doldrums. I have deliberately emphasized the word *operations* for it is not with our underlying
political philosophy that the authors disagree. Indeed, they argue that the current operational structure of government (that
is, bureaucratic) actually subverts our esteemed political ideals.

Like some others, the authors do not see reindustrialization as the cure for our economic woes. We must face facts. The
less developed countries (LDCs) have steadily stolen away old-line
labor-intensive industries from the more developed countries
(MDCs). They can produce products not only as well as we have
in the past but cheaper. There seems to be no reversing of this
trend.

The solution therefore lies not in going back to some industrial Garden of Eden that no longer exists or makes sense in
today's world but rather in going forward to the future. I quote
from the authors themselves:

> We have argued that production industries in
> MDCs are unlikely to generate a large number of
> new jobs. If jobs are to be created, they must be
> created in the service sector. The desire for services
> has been growing continuously as the standard of
> living has increased. The higher the standard of liv-
> ing, the more attention is given to the quality of
> life. Quality of life depends critically on the
> amount, availability, accessibility, and quality of
> services.
>
> However, much of the growing *desire* for
> services has not been translated into *demand* be-
> cause of their high cost, low quality, and offensive
> manner of delivery. Consequently, many jobs that
> could be created to provide desired services have
> not been. However, they can be created by de-
> creasing the cost, increasing the quality, and im-
> proving the delivery of services.
>
> The defects in services derive from the fact
> that most are provided by bureaucratic monopolies
> either within government or the private sector.
> Therefore, solving the unemployment problem lies
> in debureaucratizing and demonopolizing public

and private providers of service [Chapter Ten, page 187].

That is the thesis of this book. How the authors propose to accomplish this will and should be the focus of sharp debate. Be that as it may, two things are both clear and welcome about this book. One is that it puts in proper perspective a problem that is essentially systemic. Two, it shows that noneconomists may have more to say about so-called economic problems than do members of that profession.

Make no mistake about it. This is a radical book (I thought of Saul Alinsky many times as I read it), if by *radical* we mean *really* returning to the political ideals of our founding fathers and designing new organizational forms to make those ideals relevant to our times.

In my view, one of the best things that can be said of any book is that, whether one agrees entirely with its ideas or not, it deserves to be read and the ideas in it debated and examined. By this standard, I regard this book as being highly successful. I hope it receives the serious attention it so richly deserves.

September 1984   Ian I. Mitroff
                Harold Quinton Distinguished
                Professor of Business Policy
                University of Southern California

To Bo Ekman

*whose practices
we preach*

Preface

The prolonged recession prevailing in most Western nations has led to a number of proposals for revitalizing their economies. These proposals are generally directed at *reindustrialization* and therefore specify government measures intended to stimulate the growth of goods-producing industries. In general, these proposals try to resurrect the economic conditions of the 1960s. However, there is not a consensus on what measures are required. Moreover, many people suspect that even with economic recovery, the West will soon experience another recession. This disagreement and suspicion calls into question the effectiveness of reindustrialization strategies and the validity of the economic theories on which they are based. Such attacks on economics as the following by Stephens (1981, p. A35) are not unusual:

> The theories of economics have a dangerous artlessness. By the nineteenth century, those mak-

ing decisions on affairs of state were already en-
amored of the uncomplicated solutions offered by
economists. Only a loon would make such a statement as this: "Population, when unchecked, increases in a geometric ratio. Subsistence only
increases in an arithmetic ratio" (Thomas R. Malthus, "The Principles of Population"). Alas, our
men of influence, looking for easy ideas at a time
of disorientation caused by the Industrial Revolution grasped such twaddle and made decisions
accordingly.

The tradition of purveying ingenious solutions to intricate problems has been greatly enriched during this century. The currently fashion-
able monetarist offerings seem, if anything, even
loonier than the writings of Malthus. Imagine believing in the control of inflation by curbing the
money supply! This is like deciding to stop your
dog's fouling the sidewalk by plugging up its rear
end. It is highly unlikely to succeed, but it does kill
the hound.

Even those economists, industrialists, and politicians who
support a reindustrialization strategy do not claim that it will
solve what is probably the most serious aspect of the current
economic malaise of the West, *unemployment*. The economic
recovery they envisage does not include an equitable distribution of wealth. We believe that the ability of the goods-producing sector in more developed countries (MDCs) to produce employment is eroding because of (1) continued migration of
labor-intensive industries to less developed countries (LDCs),
(2) increased automation of those remaining in MDCs, and (3)
decreasing growth of demand for material goods in MDCs.

We also believe that the MDCs have been moving into a
new economic era, when more employment will be in the service sector. Our society has never engaged more people in the
production of goods than in the provision of services. Nevertheless, since the industrial revolution, the economies of the MDCs
have been based on production industries: manufacturing, construction, and mining; that is, the major investments and efforts
of these societies have been directed at increasing the amount
and variety of goods produced and improving their quality. The

provision of services has been seen as a costly adjunct to the production of goods.

The transformation to what many call the postindustrial revolution involves a fundamental change in a society's focus and priorities. Its major investments and efforts must be focused on increasing the amount and variety of services provided and their quality.

In the industrial era, machines that replaced the muscle of man were applied to the production of goods. In the postindustrial era, the mechanization of production will continue but the focus will be on *automation,* the use of equipment that performs mental rather than physical functions. More important, the provision of services will be increasingly mechanized and automated.

A society that makes the transition from the industrial era to the postindustrial era will give more attention to improving its quality of life than increasing its standard of living. Standard of living is a quantitative economic concept referring to the amount of material possessions; quality of life is a qualitative, aesthetic concept referring to the satisfaction we derive from whatever we have. Therefore, movement into the postindustrial era involves a transformation from an economically oriented to an aesthetically oriented society. Up to now, the service sectors of the MDCs have failed to provide the number of jobs required to solve the unemployment problem because of the generally high cost and low quality of their services and the abusive way in which many of their services are provided.

Goods-producing economies tend to regard services in general as a *cost* to industry. As a result, the provision of services is not valued as highly as material production. True, some professional services are recognized as having a vital role in national development, but even those are viewed as costs to the economy. Therefore, when the efficient provision of services is proposed as an important if not dominant objective of an economy, the reaction is likely to be very negative: The provision of service is reaffirmed as either a cost of production or a reward for successful production.

Service industries suffer as a result of their inferior status.

Historically, they have employed the least efficient segment of the work force and unprotected minorities. The small group of protected professionals aside, service personnel are generally thought of as inferior. As a result, the general quality of services has deteriorated, even though the dominant activity of goods production is losing its importance and the demand for services is increasing faster than the demand for goods. Therefore, we argue that unless MDCs learn how to provide services as efficiently and effectively as they have historically provided goods, unemployment, underemployment, and the host of social problems that attend these phenomena are bound to increase.

The provision of services will not be given its due until we stop thinking of wealth in purely monetary or materialistic terms. As long as we do, services will be perceived as wealth consuming. However, if we reconceive wealth as the net value received when we exchange one thing for another, then services can be perceived as wealth producing. For example, if the value of health care or education is perceived as being greater than the value of what we must give up to obtain them, then they increase our wealth. Such a reconceptualization of wealth implies that it is as much a matter of quality of life as of standard of living. Then wealth becomes closely identified with the good life rather than net worth.

Some countries, such as Spain and Portugal, failed to make the transition to the industrial era. Today, some Western MDCs may fail to make the transition to the postindustrial era. Therefore, one purpose of this book is to point out to leaders of governments and corporations in MDCs what they must do so that their societies can make the transition and thereby maintain, if not increase, their standard of living and improve their quality of life. Another purpose of this book is to help students understand what is going on in their societies and to determine what must be done if further progress is to be made. Finally, we also try to provide the public with such understanding and direction because we believe that a successful transformation to the postindustrial era will not be made unless the public pressures government to make it.

When the ideas expressed here were still being developed,

we discussed them with Bo Ekman, vice president of AB Volvo. He responded very positively by commissioning us to study the underlying causes of continuing unemployment; to evaluate the measures being taken to deal with it; to determine what, if anything, is additionally required of government and the private sector to solve the problem; and to identify what corporations can do to alleviate the problem and increase their ability to survive and thrive in a period of profound economic transformation. That study provided the impetus for this book, which expands on the earlier work considerably.

The reception of the original report by those industrialists, politicians, and academics who read it encouraged us to seek a wider audience. The report was thoroughly revised to make it more useful for corporate executives and managers, government officials who are in a position to affect the economy, and academics who provide both government and business with the information, knowledge, understanding, and people they require to carry out their respective tasks. Additionally, we tried to make it capable of informing and involving the public in the revitalization of our economies.

This book is divided into two parts. In the first, "From Goods to Services: Problems of Economies in Transition," we consider the nature of the problem we want to solve. In the second, "New Roles for Government—New Opportunities for Business," we consider what can be done to solve it.

Part One contains four chapters. In the first, we analyze the unemployment problem and show that current trends give us no reason to believe that the problem will solve itself. In Chapter Two we critically review the interventions by governments of MDCs to solve the problem and give our reasons for believing they cannot work. In Chapter Three we review some of the more important untried proposals for reducing unemployment, and here, too, we try to reveal their shortcomings. In Chapter Four we reformulate the unemployment problem by revealing that the best prospects for creating employment lie in the service sector; however, unless this sector imposes its efficiency and effectiveness, the prospects are not likely to be realized. The conversion of the service sector into one that is wealth producing rather than wealth consuming is the reformulated problem. We argue that its solution requires the demonopolization and debureaucratization of service providers in the public and private sectors.

Part Two contains six chapters. In the first, Chapter Five, we consider steps the government can take to demonopolize and debureaucratize the service sector, thereby improving the quality and reducing the cost of services provided. In Chapter Six we consider what corporations can do to facilitate the transition to a service-based economy and improve their own performances even if government does not act. In Chapter Seven we present six small examples that demonstrate the implementation of our proposals. In Chapter Eight we present the example of Super Fresh, a chain of supermarkets that is a subsidiary of A&P. Here a business that had died was resurrected by organizing and managing itself in ways that we suggest here. In Chapter Nine we frame an agenda for public action without which, we believe, the changes that we have proposed for government are very unlikely to be made. This agenda involves the redemocratization of Western societies. Finally, in Chapter Ten, we gather our arguments and proposals and summarize them.

We are grateful to AB Volvo, which supported the research that stimulated this book. It should be emphasized, however, that the views expressed here are those of the authors and not necessarily those of Volvo. That company is in no way responsible for the content of this work.

We are also grateful to:

Thomas A. Cowan, whose constructive criticism of this work often destroyed us;

Alexandra M. Ackoff, who translated our writing into English;

Patricia Brandt, who did our work while we worked on this manuscript; and

Joan Lonetti, who typed it, retyped it, re-retyped it. . . .

Philadelphia, Pennsylvania   Russell L. Ackoff
September 1984   Paul Broholm
                                                 Roberta Snow

Contents

Part Two: New Roles for Government—
New Opportunities for Business

The Authors

Russell L. Ackoff is Silberberg Professor of Social Systems Sciences at the Wharton School, University of Pennsylvania. He received his bachelor's degree (1941) in architecture and his doctoral degree (1947) in philosophy of science, both from the University of Pennsylvania. He holds an honorary D.Sc. degree from the University of Lancaster in the United Kingdom.

A pioneer in the fields of operations research and management science, Ackoff's current work focuses on corporate planning and problem solving. His work in research, consulting, and education has involved over 250 corporations and 50 government agencies in both the United States and abroad. He is author or coauthor of sixteen books, the most recent of which include *A Guide to Controlling Your Corporation's Future* (with J. Gharajedaghi and E. Vergara, 1984); *Creating the Corporate Future* (1981); *The Art of Problem Solving* (1978); and *Redesigning the Future* (1974).

Ackoff is a charter member and former vice-president and president of the Operations Research Society. He is also a charter member and former vice-president of the Institute for Management Science. He is a member of the American Statistical Association, the Society for General Systems Research, the Peace Science Society, and numerous other professional societies. Ackoff has received the Silver Medal of the British Operational Research Society and the George E. Kimball Medal of the Operations Research Society of America.

Paul Broholm received his bachelor's degree (1978) in philosophy from Yale University and has completed course requirements for a doctoral degree in social systems sciences at the Wharton School, University of Pennsylvania.

Broholm is author or coauthor of several articles on unemployment, microcomputers, environmental scanning, and conceptual metaphors. He has conducted organizational research at the University of Pennsylvania and at the Graduate School of Management in Delft, the Netherlands; he has also consulted with corporations in the United States and Europe. Most recently, Broholm cofounded a telecommunications company headquartered in Philadelphia.

Roberta Snow is a research associate of Busch Center at the Wharton School, University of Pennsylvania, where she has worked in research, planning, and consulting for a number of corporate sponsors. She received her bachelor's degree (1976) in linguistics and Russian and her master's degree (1978) in linguistics, both from Syracuse University; she is currently a doctoral candidate in the Department of Social Systems Sciences at the Wharton School.

Snow's research and writing has focused on the problem of economic decline and its organizational implications. Her most recent writing treats the crisis in American public education.

Revitalizing Western Economies

A New Agenda
for Business
and Government

1

The Growing Crisis of Unemployment

Despite the economic recovery proclaimed by governments of the more developed countries (MDCs) in the Western world, unemployment remains high and prospects for significantly reducing it are poor. Moreover, although the recovery is barely under way, the next recession is already being anticipated. Many people believe it to be only a short time away. Economic recovery, as it is currently understood, can no longer be assumed either to be accompanied by reduced unemployment or to be sustainable over a long period of time.

There is a widespread but erroneous belief that *reindustrialization*, revitalization of goods-producing industries, is sufficient to solve the unemployment problem. We argue to the contrary: Reindustrialization so conceived offers no promise of significantly reducing unemployment because we are entering a new economic era in which goods-producing industries will employ a decreasing portion of the work force.

MDCs are experiencing an economic transition similar in some respects to the one experienced between the eras launched by the agricultural and industrial revolutions. All Western MDCs went through the agricultural revolution, which mechanized work on the land. Mechanization in combination with the development of new seeds, pesticides, fertilizers, and farming methods significantly increased agricultural productivity, thus reducing the need for farm labor. Fortunately, this occurred

1

when industrialization, the mechanization of goods production, was beginning in urban areas. Workers coming off the land were absorbed by goods-producing and other supporting industries. The Western world entered the industrial revolution.

The agricultural revolution swept through most Western MDCs at the beginning of the eighteenth century. They began to industrialize about one hundred years later. The United States, Russia, and Japan, however, remained agrarian until the latter part of the nineteenth century and the first half of the twentieth; they industrialized rapidly and caught up with the rest of the developed world. The era spawned by the industrial revolution is now over in the MDCs.

Because of the current migration of labor-intensive industries from MDCs to less developed countries (LDCs) and increased automation of those industries remaining in the MDCs, goods-producing industries are a less and less likely source of the jobs required to reduce unemployment significantly. Unfortunately, there is no new source of jobs to absorb people cast off by the fading of the industrial era.

The end of the industrial era does not mean that fewer goods will be produced and consumed, any more than the end of the agricultural era meant that fewer agricultural products were produced and consumed. What it does mean is that fewer people will be required to produce manufactured goods. The bulk of employment will therefore have to come from non-goods-producing industries. Therefore, any opportunity to increase employment must lie in service industries. In MDCs more people are already employed in these industries than in goods production, and the base of MDC economies has shifted from goods production to the provision of services. This transformation constitutes what we call the *second industrial revolution.*

Some call it the postindustrial revolution, but because *postindustrial* implies to some the demise of industry rather than a shift of the employment base, we prefer "second industrial." Some, like Naisbitt (1982), assert that the new economy is based on information. However, because many of the new jobs do not involve information technology, we prefer the more general concept of service. Nevertheless, the changes occurring in both goods-producing and service industries are largely due to technological developments relating to the generation, processing, transmission, storage, and retrieval of information, particularly the microprocessor. Our assertions and beliefs are based on the data that follow.

Unemployment in MDCs

Unemployment in Western Europe has virtually doubled in the last five years (see Table 1). Average unemployment in

Table 1. Unemployment in Western Europe, 1978-1983.

Country	1978	1979	1980	1981	1982[a]	1983[b]
Belgium	8.4%	8.7%	9.3%	11.6%	13.9%	14.8%
Federal Republic of Germany	3.9	3.4	3.4	4.8	6.9	8.3
France	5.2	6.0	6.5	7.8	8.3	9.3
Italy	7.1	7.5	8.0	8.6	9.9	10.5
Netherlands	4.1	4.1	4.9	7.3	10.4	13.1
United Kingdom	5.7	5.3	6.9	10.2	12.2	12.5
Average	5.5	5.5	6.1	7.8	9.4	10.3

Note: Figures represent the average annual unemployment as a percentage of the civilian labor force.

[a] From European Economic Community data.

[b] Forecast.

the United States in 1984 is estimated between 7.5 and 8.0 percent, down only a trifle from a high of 9.1 percent in 1975. A short time ago unemployment of 6 percent was considered to be intolerable. The number currently unemployed is 10.6 million, which does not include people who are not working and have stopped looking for work. Their number is believed to be increasing significantly.

The number who are unemployed is much smaller than the number who have been unemployed in the recent past:

According to a Bureau of Labor Statistics survey, some 26.5 million people experienced some

> unemployment last year—22% of the labor force,
> or nearly one out of every four persons working or
> seeking work. What is more, one out of three of
> these people had at least two spells of unemploy-
> ment during the year, with an average duration of
> joblessness lasting nearly 16 weeks.
>
> All of these unemployment numbers consti-
> tute postwar records. By way of comparison, in
> 1975, which was the previous peak unemployment
> year since the Depression, only 20.2% of the work
> force experienced unemployment, and the average
> duration of a spell of joblessness was 14.2 weeks
> [*Business Week*, November 28, 1983, p. 28].

Moreover, people who are working are working less. The average
is 35.4 hours per week in the United States (1982). It was 43.5
hours in 1947, 40.5 hours in 1960, and 39.1 hours in 1970.

It is also instructive to see how employment has changed
in the three main economic sectors: agriculture, manufacturing,
and services. In 1800, 74 percent of the labor force was engaged
in agriculture; in 1900, 40 percent; in 1960, 8 percent. In 1977,
only 3 percent of all workers were engaged as farmers, farm
managers, laborers, and supervisors. Of those who worked on
farms, 25 percent were unpaid family workers.

In 1800 virtually no one in the United States was engaged
in manufacturing. By 1900, 20 percent were; by 1960, 23 percent. The peak percentage of manufacturing employment was
reached in 1920 at 27 percent. In 1900, 23 percent of all workers were employed in all production industries—manufacturing,
mining, and construction. In 1960 the percentage was the same.

In 1800, service occupations accounted for 4 percent of
those employed; in 1900, 25 percent; in 1960, 26 percent. More
recently, employment in nonagricultural production industries
went from 33 percent in 1970 to 29 percent in 1977, while employment in services (broadly conceived) went from 67 percent
to 71 percent (see Table 2).

A significant amount of the change in employment is due
to the microprocessor. According to Merritt (1982, p. 38): "Until recently capital equipment cost a good deal more than labor.
Now an industrial robot designed to do skilled work in a car as-

Table 2. U.S. Employment in Nonagricultural Industries, 1970 and 1977.

Industry	1970 (000's)	1977 (000's)
Mining	623 (1%)	831 (1%)
Contract construction	3,536 (5%)	3,844 (5%)
Manufacturing	19,349 (27%)	19,554 (24%)
Subtotal	23,508 (33%)	24,229 (29%)
Transportation and public utilities	4,504 (6%)	4,589 (6%)
Wholesale and retail trade	15,040 (21%)	18,292 (22%)
Finance, insurance, and real estate	3,687 (5%)	4,508 (5%)
Services[a]	11,621 (16%)	15,333 (19%)
Government	12,561 (18%)	15,190 (18%)
Subtotal	47,413 (67%)	57,912 (71%)
Total	70,920	82,142

[a]Includes hotel and lodging places, personal services, miscellaneous business services, motion pictures, and medical and other health services.
Source: Bureau of the Census, 1978, table 676.

sembly plant costs about $40,000. When its round-the-clock life over eight years is broken down into servicing costs and depreciation, its hourly 'wage bill' is less than $5 as opposed to the $15 earned by a Detroit worker." Twelve of the twenty-six companies listed as having more than 100,000 employees in 1970 reduced their employment by 1980. During the 1970s, Western Electric (a subsidiary of AT&T) doubled the value of its output (from $5.86 billion to $10.5 billion) while reducing its work force from 121,000 to 97,000. From 1973 to 1978, the number employed by AT&T did not change, but there were major shifts in employment reflecting the impact of information technology: The number of AT&T operators was reduced by 23 percent, and the number of directory assistance personnel, service personnel, assembly workers, and linesmen was also reduced. These reductions were offset by new jobs in sales, marketing, and management. More generally, the percentage of those employed in white-collar jobs increased from 43 percent in 1960 to 50 percent in 1977.

Services are contributing significantly more to the gross domestic product than the production of goods (see Table 3).

Table 3. Breakdown of Gross Domestic Product for Western Nations.

Country	Year	Agriculture	Goods[a]	Services[b]
United States	1979	3%	35%	62%
Austria	1980	4	40	56
Belgium	1980	2	37	61
Denmark	1977	5	25	70
Federal Republic of Germany	1980	2	48	50
France	1980	4	36	60
Italy	1980	6	43	51
Netherlands	1978	4	33	63
Sweden	1980	3	32	65

[a] Includes mining, construction, and manufacturing.

[b] Includes hotel and lodging places, personal services, miscellaneous business services, motion pictures, and medical and other health services.

Source: Bureau of the Census, 1982, table 1525.

Among the MDCs, only in West Germany are the contributions of both sectors about equal.

The Nature of New Jobs in MDCs

As previously noted, more and more jobs in MDCs are information related. According to John Naisbitt (1982):

> In 1950, only 17 percent of us worked in information jobs. Now more than 60 percent of us work with information as programmers, teachers, clerks, secretaries, accountants, stock brokers, managers, insurance people, bureaucrats, lawyers, bankers, and technicians. And many more workers hold information jobs within manufacturing companies. . . . David L. Birch of MIT reports that only 13 percent of our labor force is engaged in manufacturing operations today [p. 14] . . . .
> MIT's David Birch has demonstrated that of the 19 million new jobs created in the United States during the 1970s . . . only 5 percent were in manufacturing and only 11 percent in the goods producing sector as a whole. . . . As Birch says, "We are working ourselves out of the manufactur-

ing business and into the thinking business [p. 17]."

In the last ten years, the number of jobs in the United States has increased by 20 percent, but this has not been enough to prevent increasing unemployment. During the same period, the number of jobs in Japan increased by 10 percent, but there was no net increase in jobs in the European Economic Community (EEC). A study carried out by MIT indicates that in the United States from 1969 to 1976, 80 percent of the new jobs created were in firms with fewer than 100 employees (some of which are subsidiaries of large corporations). On the whole, employment in large corporations has been decreasing.

There is evidence that most of the new jobs created in the United States have been disproportionately low paying, requiring unsophisticated skills:

> All the fashionable talk about the need to upgrade the work force through training in computer literacy, math, science, and engineering is based on a complete misreading of economic trends. The trend is toward a deskilled and degraded work force. The work force of the future will not consist of "information workers" and "data communicators." Skilled jobs will continue to be scarce. Already many industries dependent on skilled labor have exported production to places like Hong Kong and Taiwan, where skilled labor is cheap. Other industries are replacing skilled labor with capital [Lasch, 1984, p. 45].

From 1966 to 1970, the percentage of jobs in the lowest third of the earnings distribution increased from 36 to 46 percent. Most of these jobs went to mature women and minorities and were in the service sector, which includes more small firms than the goods-producing sector. The percentage of firms with less than 250 employees is 70 percent in the service sector but 50 percent in the goods-producing sector. The supply of highly skilled workers is increasing. Although estimates vary widely, it is generally agreed that there are more college graduates in the

United States than jobs requiring their skills. Estimates of this oversupply range from 1.6 to 8.0 million.

Unemployment-Related Problems

Extended unemployment in the MDCs has created two new socioeconomic problems: the *underground* and the *underclass*.

The Underground Economy. According to Tanzi (1982, p. ix): "As is often the case with new phenomena, there is still relatively little agreement about exactly what is meant by underground economy.... For some experts, underground economy represents almost exclusively the income that is not reported to the tax authorities, regardless of whether such an income is, or is not, measured by the national accounts. For others, it is the relationship between the measured size of the economy (as estimated by the national accounts) and the actual size that is important, as the difference between total economic activity of a country and the measured part may influence economic policy in a variety of ways." We will take the underground economy to be that portion of economic activity that does not appear in the national accounts of a country.

An increasing amount of attention is being given to unrecorded economic activity, the so-called underground economy. This widespread phenomenon has a number of different names. The English call it the "hidden economy"; the Germans, *schwarzarbeit*; the French, *travail noir*; Argentinians, *morocho*; Soviets, *rabotat' nalevo*; and Italians, *lavoro nero*.

Underground economies form a significant portion of the total economies in many countries. The sizes of such economies are estimated in at least four different ways: (1) the differences between various income measures; (2) the difference between declared income and what tax authorities discover to be income after auditing; (3) the difference between the officially measured labor force participation rate and the one considered to be normal; and (4) the difference between currency normally needed and actually observed, or the difference between total and officially measured national income, given the money supply. Because these methods yield different estimates, we cannot be sure of the absolute size of any country's underground economy, but we can be reasonably sure that the size is significant. For example, in the United States it was estimated to be 27 percent of the GNP in 1979; in Sweden, between 6.9 and 17.2 percent; in Norway, between 6.4 and 16 percent in 1978; and in Australia, approximately 10 percent in 1978 and 1979.

The underground economy in the United States has been growing at an accelerating rate since the "oil crisis" of the 1970s (see Figure 1). Among the reasons cited for the growth of underground activities are the following:

1. the growth of governmental regulations, accompanied by prohibitions and reporting requirements that encourage firms and individuals to avoid costs and red tape associated with lawful employment and transactions;

2. the imposition of taxes that encourage activities to go

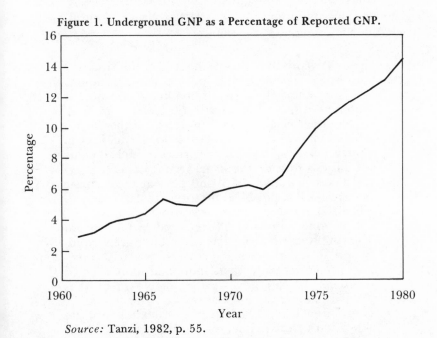

Figure 1. Underground GNP as a Percentage of Reported GNP.

Source: Tanzi, 1982, p. 55.

underground to avoid payments that seem disproportionately large compared with the income earned;

3. inflation rates that push individuals into higher tax brackets and provide an incentive to find alternative sources of income that tax collectors cannot detect;

4. the existence of loopholes in tax laws that encourage people to try to "beat the system";

5. high payments to cover human services such as unemployment, retirement, and medical care, which are often a disincentive to work in the above-ground economy;

6. the growing frustration, anomie, cynicism, and disillusionment among those who are unemployed and unable to find suitable lawful employment, all of which encourage the search for extralegal sources of support; and

7. increased leisure time resulting from reduced working hours, which is frequently used to earn extra unreported income in a second job (moonlighting).

Italy is widely thought to have the largest relative underground economy among Western MDCs. Bruno Contini (1982, pp. 200–201) described it as follows:

> Toward the end of the 1960s the situation was ripe for the revenge of the market: money wages in the official labor market could not be compressed (real wages were still lower than in all of the other neighboring countries) and therefore a parallel market for "irregular" labor services began to develop. *Irregular* is here used as a catchall name for all jobs outside the social security system (payroll taxes in Italy add 50–60 percent to the basic pay, in itself a powerful incentive to tax evasion), which are by their nature precarious, unprotected, and beyond any form of organized social control. The supply of the irregular labor force grew rapidly and so did the demand for their services. Low-paid categories of workers more and more seemed to prefer precarious forms of employment that yielded money wages below the official market rates, but allowed a high degree of flexibility in the allocation of their time, to forced inactivity. Firms

that had the option of utilizing irregular labor, either directly or by subcontracting to small-scale manufacturers, were eager to take full advantage of it.

From the demand side, the incentive to hire irregular workers to avoid payroll taxation is undoubtedly a major one. But no less important incentives include keeping the unions off limits, paying by piece-rate, and regaining unlimited flexibility of labor utilization in terms of working hours and layoffs.

Italy is also believed to have been least affected by the recent widespread recession. Some have attributed this to its large underground economy. It is not surprising, therefore, that others believe that *legal* underground economic activity offers a way to economic salvation. However, much, if not most, underground activity is not as innocent as housewives trading babysitting services or working for room and board; much of it consists of trade in drugs, gambling, and prostitution. It has been asserted that if the illegal drug trade in Florida was stopped, Florida's economy would collapse. It is impossible to encourage legal underground economic activity without doing the same for illegal activity. Moreover, because this economy yields little or no tax income for government, it imposes an inequitable tax burden on those whose activity is above ground.

A large part of underground economic activity involves barter. Although some people feel that this is a return to a noble old tradition, much of this activity is associated with corruption. Many individuals and businesses join barter exchanges to avoid taxes, and many of these exchanges have large membership fees, payable *in cash*. Some have vanished shortly after collecting these fees.

The current increase in bartering for goods and services is more a symptom of socioeconomic ills than a cure for them. Barter does not generate the capital required for investment in society's infrastructure or in the facilities and equipment required to create more jobs.

The Underclass. The decreasing number of jobs available to those entering the work force, especially those without a high school or college education, is creating an underclass, which consists of individuals who are willing to work but cannot find jobs. This class is growing rapidly in the United States, especially among minorities, and in Europe, especially in England. Even in West Germany, often cited as the strongest economy in Europe, the underclass presents a problem. According to Ulrich Borsdorf (quoted by John Vinocur, 1982, p. A1):

> There's the possibility of a new kind of class emerging, especially among young people who've never had a job, that has very little to do with the rules of society as we know them. It's impossible to say constantly growing unemployment would lead to an explosion in West Germany, but I say flatly it's a danger for the republic. . . . It's not capital versus labor anymore. It's power against no power—maybe even the people who work against those who don't.

In order to survive, those in the underclass must resort to crime, begging, welfare, or living off others. They are a burden on society or the individuals who support them, contribute nothing to society's well-being, and threaten political stability.

So much for where we have been and where we are. Now consider where we seem to be going.

Unemployment Prospects

Now that the governments of the United States and other Western MDCs have proclaimed an economic recovery, there is a widespread belief the unemployment problem will be solved. Recovery may reduce unemployment, but it cannot reduce unemployment enough to remove the problem. We are not alone in this belief. According to Giles Merritt (1982, p. 37):

> There is a time bomb inside the Organization for Economic Cooperation and Development (OECD). . . . OECD officials are pondering a prediction that by 1985 unemployment in the world's major industrialized nations will have risen to 35

million—more than twice the figure of ten years before and a third greater than today's.

Work is going to be so scarce that by the mid-1980s . . . unemployment will have become one of the most widely shared human experiences. A sixth of all Europeans will be unemployed, and a third will have had recent experience of unemployment, and the lives of 80 percent will have been touched by joblessness among friends or family.

Our lack of belief in the ability of the proclaimed economic recovery to solve the unemployment problem is based on two other beliefs: (1) that the labor force will continue to grow and (2) that the expectation of significantly more employment in mining, construction, and particularly manufacturing is not likely to be met. Consider the bases for these beliefs.

Growth of the Labor Force. The labor force will continue to grow because (1) the population will continue to grow, (2) a larger percentage of women will enter it and remain in it longer, and (3) decreasing morbidity and increasing life expectancy of workers will reduce the number of replacements and substitutes required.

Population growth. The world's population in 1982, 4.7 billion, was 25 percent larger than in 1970, 51 percent larger than in 1960, and 84 percent larger than in 1950. Conservative projections indicate that by the year 2000, the world's population will reach 6.2 billion, a 32 percent increase over the 1982 figure.

Because of different rates of population growth, in different regions of the world, the distribution of population over the last thirty years has shifted. The portion of the world's population in Africa, Asia, and Latin America (mostly LDCs) has been growing, and the portion in North America, Europe, and the Soviet Union (MDCs) has been diminishing. Of the estimated 6.2 billion people that will be inhabiting the world in 2000, 4.9 billion people will reside in LDCs. This is more than the current population of the world. In contrast, the number of people in MDCs will increase by slightly less than 10 percent, from 1.2 billion to 1.3 billion.

Even if these population trends do not continue, the size of the labor force will continue to grow dramatically through the end of the century. The large portion of the world's population born in the 1960s is just beginning to enter the work force. Those born in the 1970s will enter it in the 1990s, and those born in the 1980s after 2000. Furthermore, after these individuals enter the labor force, they will remain in it for about forty years on average. Therefore, even if there is zero population growth over the next twenty years, the labor force will continue to grow. Because most of the labor force will be located in LDCs, these countries will remain a source of relatively inexpensive labor.

Women in the work force. More women are currently entering the work force than ever before. In 1960, women made up only one third of the labor force in the United States; in 1981, they accounted for 43 percent. It is projected that they will account for almost half in the year 2000. In 1960, only 38 percent of women in the United States worked outside the home. This increased to 52 percent in 1981. In the United Kingdom and Sweden, 60 percent of the women are already in the labor force.

Decreasing morbidity and increasing life expectancy. With advances in sanitation and medicine, people are living longer. While the world's population has been increasing, death rates have been decreasing. For example, in the United States the overall death rate in 1950 was 9.6 percent; in 1981 it was 8.7 percent.

Increasing life expectancy is largely due to medicine's growing ability to cure cardiovascular diseases and disorders, the single largest cause of adult deaths. At the same time, it has become more effective in preventing and treating infectious diseases such as pneumonia, which has been a major cause of death among the elderly.

The rate of infant mortality was cut in half from 1950 to 1981. This is due to progress in diagnosing and treating perinatal diseases and congenital anomalies. For these reasons, more infants born today are expected to survive and reach old age. An American male born in 1920 had a life expectancy of fifty-five years; a female, fifty-six. In contrast, boys born in 1979 can expect to reach an age of seventy, and girls seventy-eight.

Employment in Production Industries. As previously noted, most governments of Western MDCs have tried to revitalize their economies by focusing on "reindustrialization," that is, on encouraging and facilitating the growth of production industries, particularly manufacturing. The reason for this is clear: In 1980 this sector accounted for 29 percent of those employed. Manufacturing alone accounted for 22 percent. Services employed a larger percentage, but many of these jobs exist only to support production industries and to serve those people whose incomes come from these industries. This view is reflected in a statement by Joyce Lain Kennedy (1984, p. L1): "Service jobs do not increase national wealth. . . . They simply 'move money around.' And a strong industrial base is vital for the nation's defense. So although political and industrial leaders rarely agree on anything, they do agree on the need to modernize American industry."

We do not disagree with the need to modernize American industry, but we believe that doing so will not solve the unemployment problem for two reasons: First, labor-intensive industries in MDCs will continue to migrate to LDCs, where labor costs are lower. Second, all industries, particularly those involved in production, whether troubled or not, will increasingly automate and mechanize (modernize) to maintain their competitiveness, and this will decrease their need for labor. In addition, the demand for manufactured products will not continue to increase as it has in the past because of decreasing materialism in Western MDCs. This will be discussed later in this chapter.

Industrial migration to LDCs. "Forecasts [of employment] for industrial nations pale besides those for the Third World. There are now between 300 and 500 million unemployed in the developing world; by the turn of the century the demographic figures suggest 900 million to a billion" (Merritt, 1982, p. 37). The increasing number of people entering the work force in LDCs will continue to provide labor at a low cost. This is likely to spur more migration of labor-intensive industries from MDCs. Low-cost labor has already enabled LDCs to take over more and more of the world's industrial production. According to John Naisbitt (1982, pp. 61-62):

> The twenty fastest-growing economies for the period 1970 and 1977 were *all* Third World Countries. Some were oil exporting countries— Saudi Arabia and Iran, for instance. But the vast majority were not. . . . During the past decade, the Third World has begun to take up most of the world's industrial tasks.
>
> The United States and the rest of the developed countries of the world are on their way to losing their dominant positions in industries that include steel, automobiles, railroad equipment, machinery, appliances, textiles, shoes, and apparel. . . .
>
> To the chagrin of many industrialists . . . the products of developing countries are every bit as good as those made in the industrial world—and they are cheaper.
>
> Recently, the Third World reached an important industrial benchmark. For the first time, the non-oil producing developing countries collectively exported more manufactured goods than raw materials.

Decreasing materialism. Many, if not most, consumers in MDCs are approaching or have reached saturation in their acquisition of goods. Less of their income is being spent on goods, the percentage having decreased from 59.8 percent in 1960 to 52.6 percent in 1981 (see Table 4). Conspicuous consumption by nations, organizations, and individuals is becoming an increasingly frequent target of social critics. For example, Hazel Henderson (1978, pp. 339-340) wrote:

> The cultural assumptions and economic arrangements associated with the game of "keeping up with the Joneses" are in for a dramatic reevaluation. . . .
>
> There are many levels of Jonesism. Governments indulge in an international version of it with their state airlines, and big-bang technologies, such as rockets. There is corporate and organizational

Table 4. Breakdown of Personal Consumption Expenditures.

Year	Goods[a]	Services[b]
1960	59.8%	40.2%
1965	58.4	41.6
1970	56.4	43.6
1975	55.3	44.7
1976	55.2	44.8
1977	54.5	45.5
1978	54.1	45.9
1979	53.9	46.1
1980	53.1	46.9
1981	52.6	47.4

[a]Includes both durable and nondurable goods.
[b]Includes housing, household operation, and transportation.
Source: Bureau of the Census, 1982, table 698.

Jonesism, typified by the proliferation of glittering glass skyscrapers, thick carpets, self-conscious art collections in the managerial aeries, slick cavalcades of limousines and corporate jets—all sensitively tuned to the needs of status, prestige, and display. Perhaps most interesting of all is consumer Jonesism, exquisitely interrelated with and reinforced by all the other varieties. It is here that Jonesism begins and there it may end, as our individual perceptions and values change.

The trend away from conspicuous consumption became apparent among young people in MDCs in the 1960s and 1970s. Their clothing needs were reduced to a few blue jeans and accessories. Sleeping bags, mess kits, and knapsacks replaced most furnishings. The principal luxuries in which they indulged were stereo systems and musical instruments. This generation carried its disaffection with material possessions with it into maturity, although in tempered form, and transmitted this attitude to its children and even many of its elders.

The recent recession and inflation reinforced the trend away from the consumption of goods. Contemporary writer Anne Rice ("Interview with Anne Rice," 1983, p. 69) discussed the tendency of the current generation to be more romantic and more concerned with matters of mind and spirit than with material things: "On some instinctual level we're understanding that we can no longer fulfill or express ourselves by just consuming. We can't go out and buy $4,000 worth of carpet . . . but we *can* cook a marvelous dinner and serve it elegantly. As the quantity of our lives gets limited, we turn to the quality for pleasure."

Worn out and broken possessions will, of course, be replaced, but products are being designed for longer life. Models are changing less frequently, and guarantees are being extended, as in the automotive industry. There have also been proposals to impose taxes on model changes. A 1 percent tax on model changes of consumer goods in Japan is estimated to be capable of providing the Japanese government with an income of about $1 billion each year (Jun, 1980, p. 60).

Decreasing materialism does not imply that product innovations such as pocket calculators, digital clocks, video games, word processors, and personal computers will fail to induce consumption. Invention will continue to be the mother of necessity. However, consumption of new products is not likely to offset the reduction in the consumption of old ones. All products will be less subject to trivial changes.

It is in the shift of concern from standard of living to quality of life that decreasing materialism is most clearly reflected. For example, the increase of expenditures to protect and preserve the environment in MDCs has been phenomenal. A society is not likely to become more concerned with quality of life than standard of living unless most of its members are satisfied and there are enough resources to devote to improving that quality. Put another way, concern with quality of life is only likely to dominate when the standard of living is high enough and secure enough. This is the case in Western MDCs.

For these reasons—the migration of labor-intensive industries from MDCs to LDCs, increased mechanization and automation of industries remaining in the MDCs, and a decreasing desire for goods—we do not expect reindustrialization to produce enough jobs to solve the unemployment problem.

Conclusion

Western MDCs are experiencing unemployment rates that only a few years ago were considered intolerable if not impossible, and prospects for their improvement are very poor. Obviously the unemployed are the most seriously affected. Many of them are forced to live in poverty, ironically, in lands of plenty. This increases anxiety, frustration, and anomie. The unemployed lose faith in society's ability to provide them with the economic security and quality of life they expect. Some move into the emerging underclass, which is a potential threat to social stability. Others move into the underground economy, which is both economically and politically destabilizing. This economy reduces government's ability to monitor and control economic activity in the public's interest. Moreover, it provides no capital for investing in job-creating activities.

The unemployed are an economic and moral burden on the employed and a drag on the economy. They are also a constant reminder of the waste of human resources by societies in which there is a great deal of room for improvement. Using this labor pool can provide much of this improvement. The migration of labor-intensive industries to LDCs in search of cheap labor and the modernization of those industries remaining (reindustrialization) will keep production industries from supplying the number of jobs required to reduce unemployment significantly. Unless other steps are taken, unemployment can be expected to increase. Such an increase will further reduce the need for production. Thus MDCs seem to be in a vicious cycle in which unemployment reduces the need for production and production industries must reduce their employment to survive.

For these reasons we agree with Gans (1976, p. 1): "Of all the domestic problems with which America must deal in the next few years, unemployment appears to me to be the most critical. . . . Whatever the specific programs . . . some way must be found to create and save jobs, and therefore to transform the economy into a labor-intensive direction."

The unemployment problem will not solve itself. Nor will it be solved by the economic recovery now proclaimed in the

United States and in Western Europe. Such recovery will not solve the problem for reasons already cited and later supported: Continued migration of labor-intensive production industry to LDCs in search of lower-cost labor, increased automation of the industries that remain so that they can continue to be competitive, a declining percentage of income spent on goods, and continued growth of the work force.

Solving the unemployment problem will require significant changes in the behavior of both governments and corporations. The changes required of governments, if not corporations, are not likely to be implemented without strong public pressure. Therefore, in Part Two we consider what governments, corporations, and people can do to reduce the unemployment problem.

Government, of course, is already under pressure to react to the problem. It is very difficult for elected officials to get re-elected unless they have significantly reduced high unemployment. Therefore, it is easy to explain government's efforts to do something about the problem. But why should corporations make similar efforts? There are at least four good reasons for their involvement, and as we shall see, they are compatible with corporate self-interest.

First, the unemployed consume less than the employed and hence shrink the market for manufactured goods.

Second, because of welfare payments to the unemployed, the larger the number of unemployed is, the higher the cost to government. The greater this cost is, the greater the taxes imposed on both individuals and corporations. Reduced disposable income of individuals and increased taxes also decrease the market for manufactured products. Increased taxes on corporations reduce corporate profits.

Third, workers who are threatened by unemployment understandably try to protect their jobs. Such protection often takes the form of restrictive work rules and practices that deprive employers of flexible, efficient use of their employees. Moreover, when a company's sales and production decrease, its workers tend to stretch or make work in order to forestall layoffs. In general, productivity declines with decreases in demand, and demand decreases with increases in unemployment.

Finally, and perhaps most critically, the production of goods will not offer as much opportunity for corporate growth in the future as it has in the past because of the declining percentage of disposable income spent on goods. Therefore, as we shall try to show in some detail in subsequent chapters, growth will increasingly have to come from expansion in the service industries. Because of the monopolistic hold by governments on many of the most heavily consumed services, the opportunities for such expansion critically depend on how governments behave. Therefore, corporations have a significant stake in supporting the kinds of changes in government that we propose in Chapters Five and Nine.

In the next chapter, we shall consider what governments are currently doing about unemployment and why these actions are failing to resolve the problem.

2

Why Current Strategies Are Failing

The programs that governments have used to respond to unemployment problems fall into the following five categories: (1) compensating the unemployed, (2) reducing the work force, (3) filling available jobs, (4) preserving existing jobs, and (5) creating new jobs. In this chapter we shall consider each of these in turn, focusing on their effects and the reasons for their failure to reduce unemployment.

Compensating the Unemployed

Some type of unemployment compensation is clearly needed in MDCs for political if not moral reasons. All MDCs provide such assistance, but their systems differ significantly. Many systems were improved during the late 1960s and early 1970s by extending eligibility and increasing benefits. John Vinocur (1982, p. A1) noted that "in Britain . . . the benefits for those thrown out of work go far to make up for their lack of a pay check. A similar structure of organized aid exists in West Germany, at least for workers who have had long employment records before being laid off." In the Netherlands, the minimum social benefit is set at the legal minimum-wage level. Most of the sick or out-of-work receive more, up to 75 percent of their former wages for the first two years of unemployment.

A number of these compensation programs have run into

serious financial trouble because of continuing hard times and increases in long-term and structural unemployment. As a result, in the late 1970s some governments took such steps as tightening eligibility criteria, increasing contributions by the employed and employers, taxing benefits, and attempting to cut down on abuse of the system.

Recently some public discussion has centered on the possible use of funds from unemployment insurance systems for purposes other than providing supplementary income for the jobless. A number of such uses have been proposed or introduced; providing the long-term unemployed with training financed partly from these funds, instituting job programs primarily in the public sector (workfare) financed in the same way, and allowing the unemployed to use some of their expected benefits to establish small businesses. This last measure has been implemented in France. None of these measures, however well intentioned, have significantly reduced the overall unemployment problem.

Although they alleviate the financial burdens of the unemployed, unemployment compensation programs do not solve the unemployment problem. Such compensation does not create new jobs or respond to the human costs of unemployment, which can be high in societies that place a high, even moral, value on work.

Reducing the Labor Force

Governments have taken a number of measures to reduce the labor force. If the number of people offering their labor on the market can be reduced, the unemployment rate decreases and therefore so does unemployment compensation. One way of reducing unemployment figures is to discourage those out of work from seeking work, because dropouts are not counted as unemployed. No Western government has tried to do this. Rather, they have tried to reduce the length of working life by delaying entry into the work force and accelerating retirement, by reducing the number of foreigners in the work force, and by encouraging emigration of unemployed natives.

Reducing Working Life. The labor supply can be reduced

by creating alternatives to employment for people who might otherwise join the work force, for example, by extending schooling, enlarging military forces, lowering the age of retirement, reducing the number of foreigners in the work force, and encouraging the unemployed to emigrate.

Extended schooling. Schooling, of course, has generally been extended for reasons other than employment reduction, but its impact on the size of the labor force has not been ignored. Increased schooling raises the level of competence in the labor force, but this is of economic value only if there are jobs requiring the particular competencies that have been developed. Unfortunately, this is often not the case. Moreover, there is already a surplus of college graduates in many MDCs, even though there may be shortages of people with particular skills. A surplus of well-educated individuals often leads to *underemployment*—highly trained workers employed below their level of competence. This pushes less well trained workers out of the work place and often disillusions and makes cynics of the underemployed. Estimates of underemployment vary but are unquestionably high.

Education is not an unqualified good. In a society that is not developing rapidly, increased education consumes resources that might otherwise be used to create jobs. Of course, increased schooling creates some employment, such as positions in teaching and school administration. But the ratio of students to those so employed is so high as to preclude a substantial increase in employment by extending education.

In order to attract and retain more students in schools, standards are frequently lowered. This practice puts the graduates of these schools at a disadvantage when competing for jobs against graduates from schools with higher standards. Fernando Solana, a former secretary of education in Mexico, once lamented that schools focus on producing graduates capable of filling jobs created by others rather than producing graduates capable of creating jobs for themselves and others. Not even business schools train their students to create jobs. Some offer token courses in entrepreneurship, but few schools make such courses mandatory.

In sum, although extended education has some obvious benefits, it also has some not-so-obvious deficiencies in an ailing economy. It is so expensive that even the most affluent MDCs cannot afford enough extended education to significantly reduce unemployment.

Enlarging the military. Expansion of the armed forces obviously draws actual or potential members out of the labor force, many of whom would otherwise be difficult to employ. Expansion of the armed forces is also obviously expensive. It adds to social overhead and therefore tends to be inflationary, reducing the real income of people not in the military.

Increasing the size of the military usually requires more equipment to be produced and supporting facilities to be constructed. This trickle-down effect on the economy is sometimes used to justify such expenditures, but it is only a trickle, not a flood. Unfortunately, enlarging the military is more easily justified when a country's security is threatened. Therefore, governments that want to increase defense spending find it easier to do so by generating or maintaining a threat to national security.

The relatively unproductive consumption of vast amounts of wealth by the military establishments of most MDCs raises questions about the rationality of governments. However justified such expenditures may be in the cause of defense, they are clearly not justified as a way to solve the unemployment problem. There are many more productive and more socially constructive ways to use the resources consumed by the military. Certainly improving a nation's infrastructure is one of them.

Accelerating retirement. Attempts to lower the retirement age and to induce early retirement have been widespread. Early retirement is often encouraged when layoffs are necessary, and financial inducements are frequently used. More recently, early retirement has been encouraged where unemployment of young people is particularly high. Belgium introduced a prepension system in 1976 in which a young worker had to replace each retiring worker. Other countries—for example, Denmark, France, and the United Kingdom—have also introduced early retirement schemes with the explicit objective of making jobs available for young people. In these programs, how-

ever, a young worker is not required to replace the displaced
older one. There is no evidence that these schemes have significantly reduced unemployment even among the young.

Moreover, early retirement can have detrimental effects.
It requires supporting the retired for a longer period, and it generally costs more to support them than young unemployed
workers. Early retirement also often replaces experienced,
skilled workers with less experienced and less skilled ones. And
despite significant resources devoted to many plans to reduce
youth unemployment, recent evidence indicates that it is higher
than ever, and that the gap between the unemployment rate for
youth and that for the entire labor force has been growing. Finally, and most important, even if early retirement schemes
achieved their stated goals, they would still be nothing more
than job redistribution schemes—when it is new jobs that are
needed.

Reducing the number of foreigners in the work force.
Most MDCs strongly encouraged workers to immigrate from less
developed countries during the prosperous 1960s and early
1970s. Indians and Pakistanis poured into England, Turks into
Germany, and Mexicans and Puerto Ricans into the United
States. Foreign workers without papers have been essential to
the construction and agricultural industries in southern France
and play a major role in the economies of Texas and California.

However, most MDCs now severely limit the inflow of
foreign workers, and many encourage resident foreign workers
to return to their native countries. France has repeatedly offered payment to guest workers who are willing to return to
their homes. Such measures have not been successful, though,
and legal and illegal immigration to MDCs continues.

Since foreign workers usually have even less chance for
employment in their homelands than in their host countries,
and since unemployment benefits in their homelands are usually
less generous, if they exist at all, most foreign workers are unwilling to return home. Furthermore, if foreign workers were to
return to their homes en masse, some allied less developed countries would be thrown into economic and even political chaos.

Furthermore, in European countries where the minimum

wage almost equals the minimum level of welfare payments, many jobs are unacceptable to natives and would go begging were it not for willing guest workers. Even today such workers are often required to fill menial service and demanding production jobs that unemployed natives are unwilling to take.

Encouraging the emigration of unemployed natives. A number of less developed and undeveloped countries have tried to reduce their labor force by encouraging their unemployed to emigrate to more prosperous countries. This has been the case in Mexico, Turkey, Portugal, and Morocco. Of course, such emigration neither creates nor saves jobs.

The money sent home by emigrant workers is generally helpful and sometimes essential to the economies of their native countries. However, these workers often face severe social problems in their host countries. The jobs available to these workers are generally low paying and the least desirable to natives. As a result, visiting workers tend to have low status and to maintain a poor quality of life. They are usually forced to live in segregated enclaves and become the target of discrimination.

As unemployment rises in a host country, guest workers are increasingly resented. French political parties on the right have tried to stimulate and exploit such resentment by equating the two million foreign workers with the two million unemployed French. There have been demonstrations and organized protests directed against foreign workers in the Netherlands, Germany, and Norway, as well as France.

Whatever the benefits LDCs derive from exporting their unemployed to MDCs, MDCs have not found an effective way to induce these people to return home. It is almost impossible to create incentives that induce such reverse migration.

Filling Available Jobs

Governments of MDCs have tried to reduce unemployment by locating and filling available jobs. They have done so by (1) setting up placement services, (2) training workers to fill existing or anticipated jobs, and (3) subsidizing the relocation of workers to places where jobs are available.

Placement Services. There are some unfilled jobs in every economy no matter how much unemployment there is. This is partly a consequence of the lack of information about available jobs. Recognizing this, several countries have improved their public employment services. They have increased the staffs of placement agencies, improved the training of staff personnel, introduced compulsory notification by employers of vacancies, initiated self-service placement facilities, and extended the availability of vocational guidance. "Job markets" and "job fairs" have been organized in the Netherlands, Belgium, and the United States; some countries have also set up publicly run temporary work agencies or special offices that deal with temporary employment.

Such measures have not had a large impact on unemployment, nor can they be expected to do so. The number of job openings currently available in most MDCs is small compared with the number of unemployed, and the people looking for work often lack the skills for many of the available jobs. This mismatch suggests the need for training the unemployed, another measure widely used.

Training. Most MDCs have taken steps to train or retrain workers in order to prepare them for particular jobs for which there is an actual or anticipated demand. Some governments have created public programs for this purpose; others provide employers with incentives for engaging in such training and retraining. Japan, West Germany, and the United States, among others, subsidize employers to cover all or some of the costs involved. Such government programs often focus on workers who have been unemployed for some time, for example, the American Comprehensive Employment and Training Act (CETA). Some programs focus on young unemployed. Others induce companies not to lay off current employees but to retrain them.

Some small-scale programs are aimed at providing workers with high-level skills that are required for hard-to-fill vacancies, for example, Australia's "Skills in Short Supply" program, initiated in 1978. In this program financial assistance is provided to companies to cover the costs and wages required to train people for selected highly skilled occupations. The United Kingdom has had specialist training programs in computer-related occupations, offshore oil operations, and other highly skilled occupations.

Training and retraining programs have helped some workers, but not many compared with the number of unemployed. Such programs cannot have a large impact on unemployment unless the number of jobs available for trained personnel is almost as large as the number of unemployed. This has not been the case.

Subsidizing the Relocation of Workers. Work opportunities are never distributed equally over a country, and unemployed workers do not always live where jobs are available. In addition, workers tend to be less mobile when an economy is not performing well. For these reasons, a number of governments have tried to relocate some of their unemployed. For example, New Zealand introduced an "Inter-District Job Contract Scheme" in 1977, in which persons registered as unemployed for four weeks or longer were provided with nonrefundable return fares for interviews in other districts. They also received assistance with moving expenses. France has had a special mobility incentive for young people unable to find a first job near their place of residence.

Measures to encourage worker mobility have had little impact on unemployment. Not the least problem has been the reluctance of the unemployed to move away from family and friends from whom they derive some financial and a good deal of moral support. Moreover, housing shortages have also impeded worker mobility. Amsterdam has 53,000 people officially registered as in urgent need of accommodations. Throughout the Netherlands, housing regulations make it hard to get a place to live unless one has lived in an area for years.

Moreover, mobility programs do not guarantee jobs in a new location. Anecdotes of the migration from Detroit to the Sun Belt tell of families returning home because they could not find jobs or housing or because they could not afford to live on the welfare benefits they received while looking for jobs. Newspapers have carried stories of families with children having to live in automobiles while the father unsuccessfully looked for work. Little wonder the unemployed are reluctant to move.

Preservation of Existing Jobs

To prevent unemployment from increasing, every MDC has tried to preserve existing jobs. Measures directed to this end have been of three types: (1) protectionist reduction of foreign competition, (2) discouraging or prohibiting layoffs, and (3) subsidizing employers or demand for their outputs.

Protectionism. "With unemployment increasing in the EEC countries, protectionism likely will continue to rear its head in one form or another even as countries denounce the policy in principle" (Rangachari, 1982, p. 42). The principal objective of protectionism is to protect domestic industries and jobs from foreign competition, particularly in infant or large, declining industries. Protectionism has many forms, the most common of which are the following:

1. "Voluntary agreements" with foreign countries that limit their exports. Such agreements are usually induced by threats of such retaliative measures as imposing or increasing tariffs or withdrawing aid. Both the United States and the EEC have been pressuring Japan to restrict its exports. During a visit to Tokyo, Prime Minister Margaret Thatcher of Great Britain ironically told her hosts that the imbalance in Western trade with Japan could not continue without causing a breakdown of the international system of free trade. At this writing the government of the United States is under considerable pressure from steel companies and related unions to strengthen protectionist barriers against European as well as Japanese competition.
2. Import duties. These are most commonly imposed where foreign goods are believed to be subsidized and therefore unfairly competitive. Such duties are often initiated by "trigger-price mechanisms." When imported goods fall below a price believed to be fair, countervailing duties are imposed.

3. Restrictive content rules on imported products. Specified imported products, such as automobiles, are not allowed to be sold in the domestic market unless a specified percentage of their contents have been produced domestically.

4. Requirements that government agencies purchase only domestically produced goods if they are available.

5. Extralegal obstructions to importing. Governments that proclaim support of free international trade are often reluctant to take formal steps against countries exporting to them. They prefer informal measures, for example: "In France, where there is much talk about 'the reconquest of the domestic market,' the government has placed restrictions on video record-players, making it necessary to send them for inspection to the small city of Poitiers—roughly the equivalent of requiring all wines imported by the United States to pass through a customs shed in Des Moines" (Vinocur, 1982, p. A1).

There are many disadvantages to protectionism. Even economists who seldom agree on anything agree on its undesirability.

> Economists agree that curtailing free trade will spell doom for the world's economies. But the argument does not prevent the hardest-hit industries from seeking protection for their products.
>
> Even for the United States, which is more self-sufficient than most countries, trade has become increasingly important. . . .
>
> But this has not stopped the United States from seeking to curb imports of Japanese automobiles, European steel, textiles, and sugar. And now Congress is considering legislation that would require virtually all automobiles sold in the United States to be built substantially of parts made in the United States. Other countries have been taking similar actions [Arenson, 1982, p. A1].

Protectionism stimulates inflation by forcing the purchase of goods from other than the least-expensive supplier. Higher-

than-necessary prices reduce real income, which in turn reduces
spending and saving. This results in fewer jobs and less output
than there would otherwise be. Perhaps the most serious deficiency of protectionism is the fact that it tends to preserve inefficient industries and retard their modernization.

> Skeptics who think this is so much theoreti-
> cal eyewash should consider. . . . Between 1968
> and 1974, and then again since 1978, American
> steel companies have been largely protected against
> imports of Japanese and European steel. The pro-
> tection was supposed to give them a chance to im-
> prove their efficiency. It did exactly the opposite.
> This year, those cossetted steel-makers are produc-
> ing steel that . . . is up to 50% more expensive than
> the Japanese equivalent. American steel *users* com-
> peting against the Japanese have therefore been
> handicapped ["World Economy Survey," 1983, p.
> 17].

No wonder the American auto companies, the largest consumers of American steel, are at a competitive disadvantage
with the Japanese. (However, this is not the only reason.) Their
disadvantage has generated the proposed domestic content legislation on automobiles and the "voluntary agreement" by which
Japan limits its exportation of automobiles in the United States.
This agreement was quickly imitated by European countries.
One result was the decision by Nissan *not* to construct a new
plant in Great Britain that would have employed more than
5,000 people directly and many more indirectly.

Protectionism encourages foreign exporters to upgrade
their products in order to maintain their earnings. They begin
to address specialized and more affluent segments of the market where protectionist measures do not apply. As a result,
the value of imports is often not reduced by nearly as much
as the quantity.

In some cases a foreign company can evade protectionism by exporting from one of its plants in a nonrestricted
country; on the other hand, a foreign plant of a domestically
owned company may be prevented from exporting to its home

country. Moreover, such restrictions inevitably invite retaliation by affected countries.

Perhaps most important is the fact that protectionism discourages protected domestic industries from improving their productivity. Instead, it promotes their diversification. To a large extent they diversify by acquiring other companies, which displaces development as the principal path to growth. Acquisition, unlike internal development, tends to reduce the number of jobs, not increase them.

Extensive research has shown that even LDCs can suffer from closing their borders to imports. The temptation is obvious: Buy at home, build up domestic industries, and create local jobs. But the resulting distortion of prices can have harmful consequences throughout the economy. This is reflected in the fact that a "distortion index" has been developed; its use reveals a high correlation between price distortion (prices that do not accurately reflect the value of goods produced) in an economy and low growth of gross domestic product.

"Fixing" Employment. Some governments—for example, those of Japan, Sweden, and West Germany—have made it very difficult or costly to terminate the employment of workers who have survived a probationary period. Throughout the OECD, since the 1960s there has been a marked rise in dismissal costs and in related nonwage labor costs, such as that for unemployment insurance. This has tended to reduce the ability of the labor market to adjust to changing conditions. It has also obstructed the entry of young people into the labor market because of the increased cost of hiring them and of firing older workers. The cost of labor, once completely variable, has become increasingly fixed. As a result, when management needs additional labor, it is inclined to use overtime rather than add employees. It is also driven to mechanize and automate new production rather than use labor for it. At best, fixing employment protects existing jobs; it not only does not create new ones but actually discourages such creation.

Subsidies. Governments have provided a wide variety of subsidies for employment. Such assistance to industries, whether temporary or long term, has been aimed at creating new jobs as well as preserving old ones. It has taken several forms: (1) wage subsidies, (2) subsidies for those partially employed, (3) subsidies of demand, and (4) subsidies to support improvements or survival of firms in trouble. Nationalization has often been used as the ultimate form of subsidization.

Wage subsidies. The governments of Sweden, the United Kingdom, and Japan, among others, have provided this type of subsidy. In Japan these subsidies have been used to facilitate the restructuring and modernization of an industry, during which employers are encouraged to maintain employment levels. This is compatible with Japan's general strategy of increasing the viability of private enterprises without absorbing the unemployed in the public sector. The United Kingdom, on the other hand, has traditionally applied no pressure on subsidized firms to restructure, modernize, or retrain employees.

Wage subsidies have usually been offered to industries that are in financial trouble. Most industries in MDCs that have received such subsidies—with Japanese firms being notable exceptions—have not effectively transformed or modernized themselves, but their lives have been extended. Wage subsidies tend to delay rather than accelerate restructuring and modernization. Without such changes jobs may be preserved by subsidies, but they are not created. Without increased productivity, prices remain unnecessarily high and the consumer pays.

Subsidies for the partially employed. Benefits to cover reduced time at work and part-time employment have been offered by governments in Europe and Japan. Such subsidies are based on the belief that partial unemployment benefits are less expensive than total unemployment benefits. In West Germany, on occasion, there have been about as many people on short-time work as were unemployed. In France, financial aid to workers who are partially employed dates back to the 1960s. In 1975 France enacted a law that encouraged firms to reduce the number of redundant employees by introducing short-time work. This was the conservative government's forerunner of the socialist government's move toward mandatory reduction of the work week. In accordance with the law of 1975, France's National Employment Fund paid up to 80 percent of the earnings lost by those who were partially employed.

In some cases, subsidies of the partially employed are linked with training intended to increase the recipients' skills. Whether or not such subsidies are linked with retraining, they have been used more to aid ailing industries than to support ones with growth potential. They encourage the reduction of full-time employment to part-time, not the addition of part-time employees.

Subsidies of demand. Governments have tried to preserve jobs by subsidizing the income received by producers of goods and providers of services. Direct subsidies—outright payments to a private firm for producing or not producing—are less common than indirect subsidies because they are less palatable politically. Some governments guarantee to purchase specified amounts of certain products at a price that enables their producers to remain in business. For example, in the United States the privately operated airlines are subsidized by their being paid for transporting mail.

Governments often provide support by purchasing and stockpiling goods in order to maintain high levels of production. This is the intention of the Common Agricultural Policy of the EEC. Other countries have similar practices. Producers may be guaranteed a minimum price for some or all of their output. In addition, prices to consumers can be kept low through subsidies, thus protecting producers from the inability of consumers to purchase the producers' goods. CONASUPO, the National Basic Commodity Agency in Mexico, subsidizes farmers to maintain production and then keeps the prices of their products to consumers low enough to maintain demand for them.

Governments sometimes pay producers to produce. This has been the main thrust of agricultural policy in the United States for years. Price subsidies do not increase productivity or make producers more competitive. In fact, they discourage such improvements. They can increase consumption by many who could not otherwise afford the subsidized products, as in Mexico's food program. But such subsidies are costly, and their price is paid one way or another by people who can afford to pay. Subsidies do protect some existing jobs but do not create new ones. Whatever benefits they produce, reduced unemployment is not one of them.

Rescues. Some governments of MDCs try to bail out large industrial employers who are about to go bankrupt. Their purpose is to protect employment. This was the case when the American government assisted Lockheed and Chrysler, when Belgium gave support to its steel industry, and when the Dutch government came to the aid of DAF (now a part of Volvo). Various types of support are offered, including guaranteeing loans made to the company by private sources, lending government money, and providing purchase agreements. Rescue operations are usually justified by the argument that the cost to the public of providing unemployment benefits to people who would be thrown out of work by the company's closing exceeds the cost of keeping the company afloat. However, rescues are often motivated more by political considerations than economic. This is particularly apparent where the operations involved are the government's. For example, the inefficient Philadelphia Navy Yard, like many other old government installations, is kept in operation because of political pressures by local politicians and the fear of elected government officials of losing local support at the polls. This is reflected in former Vice President Mondale's attack on opponent Sen. Gary Hart in the Michigan primaries. Mondale accused Hart of not having supported aid to Chrysler, which employs many people in Michigan.

The obvious deficiency of rescues is that they help weak companies survive. Chrysler recovered, but most rescues have not had such salutary results. For example, France is still massively subsidizing its national steel companies. The only hope seen by the current government is widespread reduction of the labor force and plant capacity. The resources consumed by such subsidies might well have more beneficial effects on a nation's economy if they are used to develop companies with good prospects for growth.

Nationalization. Nationalization is the ultimate form of government subsidy. Spain recently nationalized the large Rumasa group to keep it from going under. The postwar Labor government in Great Britain nationalized the coal and steel industries as a matter of political policy, but they have been administered through succeeding governments and have lost increasing amounts of money.

Nationalization is a seemingly simple way to gain control of the resources required to run an economy well and to preserve jobs. Unfortunately, it has seldom worked this way. If one examines the recent conversions to public ownership of formerly profitable enterprises in Mexico and Portugal, for example, it is apparent that their profitability has almost always decreased. The jury is still out on recent French nationalizations, but the record is very mixed on other French state-owned companies. Renault has done reasonably well, but the steel companies have performed badly. In general, no government has been able to manage an industrial sector under nationalization better than the private sector.

Creating New Jobs

Increasingly, new jobs are seen as the only solution to the unemployment problem. New jobs are a sign of a healthy economy. They offer a future to those seeking work and preserve political stability. Unfortunately, it is not easy to create new jobs, especially with limited resources. There are a number of government strategies that are intended to overcome these difficulties. These include: (1) increasing public employment, (2) inducing increased private employment, (3) work sharing, and (4) attracting potential employers.

Public Employment. Perhaps the easiest and most tempting way for a government to create employment is to expand itself. It is certainly the policy with the fastest, most visible, and most direct results. In the United Kingdom, for example, there is a long tradition of creating jobs in the public sector when jobs are needed. In the 1970s the British government enlarged the legislative base, permitting it to increase legally mandated employment programs in the public sector. In 1975 and 1977 there was a similar enlargement of the legislative base in the United States: CETA. At this program's peak in 1978, it provided employment for 1.2 million people. Only a limited number of these additional jobs were created in the normal parts of the public sector or through public works. As was done in Canada, many of these jobs were used to support local initiatives.

Similar programs have been put in place in Denmark, Finland, the Netherlands, New Zealand, and Norway. Some countries, such as France and the Netherlands, initiated programs to create short-term public jobs in the normal parts of the public sector, but the scale of such programs has generally been small. In some countries people have been employed in the public sector to provide assistance to the unemployed or otherwise needy. In Sweden, for example, about 50,000 were so employed in 1978-1979, when only about 45,000 unemployed were registered in the country.

Public employment programs are usually short-lived. People employed in them and their employers know this. This breeds a casual attitude toward the work provided, even when it has an important social function. Many of the jobs created are intended to meet important social needs, but the impermanence of such programs tends to reduce their effectiveness. They are usually poorly administered and organized, and they tend to try to please the sources of their support more than those who are supposed to benefit from the services provided.

The experience and skills obtained by people employed in these programs are seldom transferable to more permanent jobs. Although these programs create jobs, they do not increase society's ability to create productive jobs or to employ people productively.

Inducing Private Employment. Governments have also tried to induce the private sector to create new jobs. Subsidies have been offered to firms that increase their work force. France, for example, has made significant efforts of this type. It introduced such a program in 1975 (*prime d'incitation à la création d'emplois*), which was followed by a series of "national employment pacts" that promoted the employment of young people and, in later versions, of other designated groups. Sweden offered substantial subsidies for new jobs created in 1978-1979. Unless private employers in such programs are closely monitored, some try to replace existing jobs with subsidized ones.

Various tax and fiscal measures are used to encourage the creation of new jobs. Both Canada and the United States have offered tax credit programs to firms that expanded their employment. Even local governments and private enterprises have participated in such programs; the Philadelphia Electric Company has offered reduced utility rates to customers who expand their employment. Perhaps the most effective inducement offered by governments has been marginal employment subsidies to growing firms, intended to reduce their cost of expanding.

New jobs created by subsidies are likely to disappear when the subsidies do. But the principal difficulty with programs to induce employment is that there may not be enough demand to justify increased production and thus to generate additional employment. If there is enough demand to justify more employment, inducements are not necessary. Therefore, it is not surprising that these programs have had little impact on unemployment. France, perhaps the most aggressive subsidizer of job creation, has nevertheless suffered a steadily increasing rate of unemployment.

Work Sharing. Work sharing is a deceptively attractive way of trying to increase employment. It seems to be supported by simple arithmetic: If, say, 10 percent of the work force is unemployed, then a proportional reduction of the time spent at work by those who are employed should create enough jobs to put all the unemployed to work. Unfortunately, things are not this simple. Efforts to divide jobs and wages between two workers run into difficulties. More workers doing the same amount of work usually requires more shifts, and extra shifts can increase lost time. Further, since some social security and benefit payments by employers are made at a flat rate, taking on additional workers increases total labor costs even when it does not increase total wages. But it usually does increase wages; employed workers are reluctant to accept a decrease in wages proportional to the decrease in their working time. Employers are equally unwilling to pay the same wages for fewer hours. When President Mitterand of France promised to cut the work week from forty to thirty-five hours, employers protested paying the same wages for less work. Reacting to a similar proposal made in West Germany, employers argued that level wages for less work would be a strong incentive to reduce employment.

Belgium and France have legislated a one-hour reduction in the official work week, from forty to thirty-nine without noticeably reducing their unemployment. The Netherlands, among other countries, has introduced work sharing in the public sector in an effort to create part-time jobs but without marked effect.

The working time of industrial workers in MDCs has been reduced by about one third since the beginning of this century. This was made possible by more-than-compensating increases in their productivity, much of which derived from technological improvements. Without productivity improvements, reduced working hours must be accompanied by reduced wages if employers are to survive in a competitive economy.

Finally, it should be noted that in today's economy, work sharing has more impact on the distribution of income than on the amount of income distributed.

Attracting Potential Employers. Governments of nations and of states and municipalities try to encourage companies to open new facilities or not to close existing ones in their jurisdictions. Within the United States, for example, cities and states often bid against each other in efforts to lure new facilities. Among the incentives offered are tax rebates, guaranteed loans (often with low interest rates), direct government subsidies, and relief from various taxes and regulations.

However, relocation usually results in a net loss of jobs and is often done for just this purpose. It rarely produces a net increase in jobs. In 1982, International Harvester induced Springfield, Ohio, and Fort Wayne, Indiana, into a bidding war to determine in which city the company would consolidate operations that were then divided between the two. The consolidation resulted in a net loss of jobs, and the bidding extracted a substantial subsidy from Springfield.

Bigger news stories and more jobs derive from international competition for the production facilities of multinationals. National policy in Taiwan and Singapore keeps wages low and the business climate attractive in order to lure production facilities from the United States and Europe. India advertises its high-technology export zone (SEEPZ), in which multinationals can operate free from many Indian regulations and taxes.

Common Market trade barriers have persuaded many multinationals to locate production facilities in an EEC country, and member nations often compete fiercely for such facilities. When Ford recently planned a new European plant, it received bids from Austria, Spain, and the United Kingdom that promised tax benefits, cooperative and plentiful labor, and other enticements. The British government recently offered government aid worth $7.5 million to the Japanese tool maker Yamazaki to build a plant in England, and the Britain Scottish Development Agency has offered National Semiconductor, the American electronics firm, 25 to 30 percent of the cost of a planned expansion in Greenock, Scotland.

The De Lorean Motor Company case illustrates some of the pitfalls of this approach to job creation. The British government saw De Lorean's proposal to build a new car-producing facility as a big opportunity to create jobs in economically depressed Northern Ireland. The government was so anxious to succeed that it lost its sense of objectivity, paying about $50,000 for every job created. The plant was built but had a very short life. However, even if it had not closed, the government would have been unlikely to recover its investment from wage taxes, reduced unemployment costs, and other revenues.

The possibility of quick, one-shot creation of a large number of jobs is very seductive. But even under the best of circumstances, there can be several flies in this ointment. First, the new jobs are often, but not always, jobs lost elsewhere. Springfield's victory was Fort Wayne's loss. In some cases, many of the jobs in a newly located facility are filled by workers who have moved from the community with the closed facility. This considerably reduces the number of jobs available in the new location. Even when new jobs are created, beneficial effects are usually confined to a small area and are modest compared with local needs. Moreover, there are a limited number of such relocations or new locations, too limited to solve the unemployment problems of many jurisdictions.

Second, the costs of the enticements, benefits, and concessions absorbed by jurisdictions often do not justify the results; they are too high. Unfortunately, they are often successful politically even though they fail economically.

Finally, over the long term, the concessions and benefits expire, and the facility must increase its productivity. This often occurs at the expense of some of the jobs created.

Conclusion

We have considered most of the ways by which governments have been trying to reduce unemployment or prevent its increase. It is only too apparent that these measures, separately or collectively, have not succeeded. However, the reasons for their failure are not so apparent.

The jury is still out on the efficacy of various subsidies to industry and on such questions as the ideal level of unemployment compensation. Debates on these issues, however, are attempts to fine-tune a system that has fundamental problems. After half a decade of various job-saving and job-creating measures, the unemployment rates in the major developed economies (twelve countries) were over 8.0 percent. Five of these had unemployment rates over 11.2 percent. Exceptions included Sweden, which employed more people in unemployment relief than were registered as unemployed, and Switzerland, where guest workers are summarily deported in difficult times. Most of the measures taken by governments in the developed Western economies have served only to redistribute existing jobs. If any jobs have been saved by such measures as trade barriers, the cost has been far higher than offering unemployment compensation at 100 percent of the lost job. Such resource-consuming measures impoverish the national economy and run the risk of sparking trade wars with devastating international results. Solving the problems facing Western economies does not lie with the measures undertaken to date.

Most of the measures taken by governments are directed at protecting existing jobs rather than creating new ones. Most of these have helped enterprises that are not competing effectively in a free market. Therefore, government programs have provided a disincentive to such redesign of these enterprises to increase their viability, let alone to create new jobs.

Measures directed at creating new jobs are generally excessively expensive and have had little effect. What effect they have had has mostly been short-term.

Most of the job-preserving and job-creating measures taken by governments involve efforts to change the behavior and structure of enterprises; none are directed at changing the behavior and structure of government. This is not surprising, since government has taken the initiative. But, as we shall try to show, the unemployment problem derives from how governments and corporations *interact*. To set this interaction right, governments as well as private enterprises will have to be redesigned.

Governments have not suffered from lack of advice. Much of the advice offered has been ignored because of its sheer volume and contradiction. However, this does not mean that the advice offered does not contain a solution to the unemployment problem. For this reason, in the next chapter we shall review some of the more prominent proposals that have been put to governments.

3

Shortcomings
of Proposed Solutions

We have already pointed out that many people believe that economic recovery, which they assume to be inevitable, will solve the unemployment problem, and therefore nothing need be done to correct it. Others who do not believe that recovery is inevitable think that interventions are necessary to bring the recovery about, which will then solve the unemployment problem. Only a few people are of the opinion that real, as opposed to apparent, economic recovery is not possible without first solving the unemployment problem.

Clearly, the meaning of economic recovery is in question. Most people identify it with an acceptable rate of growth in the GNP. A few raise questions about the appropriateness and suitability of this measure of economic performance, pointing out that the GNP can improve in the current environment while unemployment gets worse.

Those people who believe that intervention is necessary, whatever their reasons, have produced a large number of proposals, most of which fall into four categories:

1. dialogue—initiating discussions that will generate ways to bring about economic recovery;
2. industrial policy—implementing cohesive economic measures directed at reindustrialization, the growth of production industries;
3. political-economic reform—reformulating social objectives

and making the political as well as the economic changes required to realize them; and
4. radical transformation—changing the social-political-economic system to fit a new conception of what society should be.

A variety of proposals lie within each of these categories, but there is little agreement among them. Because the number of proposals is large, we have selected for consideration here some that are prominent and representative. We do not describe them in detail; rather, we focus on their underlying assumptions because we believe them to be faulty.

Dialogue

Some people believe that if knowledgeable representatives of each sector of the economy can come together, they will come up with solutions to our economic problems. For example, Rep. Timothy Wirth of Colorado recently introduced a bill in Congress that would establish a National Economic Cooperation Council "to improve collection and use of economic data, to promote cooperation among government, business and labor, and to promote consensus economic policies" (Irons, 1983, p. 49).

The sentiment behind this bill is sound, but there is little reason to believe that even a high-powered discussion group can accomplish anything of value in the fractious American political arena. Nor is there any assurance that any good ideas the proposed council did come up with would be implemented. There have been many such groups in the past, most of them long forgotten. Recall President Nixon's National Commission on Productivity, which, according to Stein (1983, p. 65) persisted in "innocuous desuetude" long after its failure became clear. This is only one example among many; others are the National Advisory Commission on Intergovernmental Relations, the Commission on Industrial Innovation, the Commission on Federal Paperwork, the President's Private Sector Survey on Cost Control, and the National Commission on Excellence in Education.

It is unlikely that advisory commissions, councils, or

committees established at any level of government will solve problems like those facing Western economies. Bringing labor, business, and government leaders together, with or without representatives of the public, is more a way of protecting the status quo than of creatively solving the unemployment or any other economic problem. The experience of President Nixon's National Commission on Productivity supports such skepticism. At the first meeting of this commission, George Meany, then president of the AFL-CIO, "made it perfectly clear that he did not intend to discuss either wages or ways to get more out of workers" (Stein, 1983, p. 65). Similar conservatism on the business side can be elicited by proposing that workers be seated on corporate boards.

National committees, commissions, and councils are usually made up of representatives of big industries and big unions, both often in a declining state. Smaller organizations with growth potential are seldom represented. The constituencies represented are usually conservative, pressuring their representatives to keep things as they are. Innovative and unconventional ideas, if proposed, are usually set aside without serious evaluation, dismissed as "politically infeasible." Such groups are more concerned with what they believe *can* be done than with what they believe *ought* to be done. Unfortunately, effective solutions to complex problems seldom appear feasible when proposed; they must be made feasible by persistent, committed, and courageous advocates. Individuals inclined to such advocacy are seldom asked to serve on policy-advising groups.

Despite the preceding negative comments, we have no principled opposition to dialogue. To the contrary, we believe that relevant and effective dialogue between the right parties is very much needed; however, there are questions. What kind of dialogue is relevant? Who should be involved in it? How can it be conducted so that its recommendations have a good chance of being implemented? How can its effective implementation be assured? Our own proposals, set forth in Chapters Five, Six, and Nine respond to these questions. Our response is based on two beliefs. First, a dialogue confined to *any* elite cannot lead to a solution of any societywide problem. Second, the kind of dialogue required is one in which *everyone* who can be affected by the implementation of its conclusions has an opportunity to participate.

Industrial Policy

Eizenstat. Stuart Eizenstat (1984), former domestic policy advisor to President Carter, pointed out that every president since George Washington has made economic decisions and that these, taken together, constitute a national *industrial policy*. Given the fact that such a policy exists, Eizenstat argues, why not recognize and rationalize it, thereby making it more efficient and effective? His proposals include the following:

1. establishing a job training program as part of a movement away from welfare payments and toward an integrated national employment and training system,
2. expanding government support for research and development, and
3. instituting a tripartite board—labor, management, and government—to serve as a forum for a national dialogue directed at producing consensus on industrial policy.

Eizenstat and others make an important point when they assert that not only is industrial policy made but it cannot be avoided. Therefore, there is a strong appeal to the idea that the decisions which in the aggregate form the policy ought not to be made in an ad hoc way. They should be made as integrated parts of a rational strategy. It is not obvious, however, that a rational policy will have better effects on American industry than an irrational one.

Rationality is a subjective, not an objective, criterion. What appears rational to one person often appears irrational to another. Then whose concept of rationality is to be used? That of Eizenstat's tripartite board? Who is to guarantee its rationality? It would be foolish to assert that such a board cannot come up with an effective policy, but the past record of similar bodies gives little cause for optimism. Such boards have clarified the consequences of current policies and identified ways of implementing them more efficiently. But if these policies are ineffective, improving their implementation only makes things worse.

Should an advisory board recommend a cohesive policy, it would have little chance of being implemented intact. Legislators make decisions, not policies. They reduce policy recommendations to sets of discrete decisions, each of which is formulated, debated, and modified separately. The cohesiveness and effectiveness of the original policy recommended are almost always lost in the process.

As for Eizenstat's proposals for a national training and employment system and expanded government support for research and development: The former cannot create jobs, and although the latter can, it cannot do so for some time to come. If rationalization means the creation of a consistent set of policy-forming decisions that effectively achieve explicitly formulated objectives that are accepted by consensus, one could hardly take issue with a proposal for it. However, we do not believe that Eizenstat's proposals are likely to produce such policies and, if by some chance they did, that they are likely to be implemented effectively. Therefore, the question we must face is: How can a *process* of rationalization be designed so that it has a reasonable chance (1) of producing effective and internally consistent policies and (2) of implementing these effectively? Again, we try to answer this question in Chapter Nine.

Magaziner and Reich. Many advocates of an explicitly formulated industrial policy do not believe that specifying ways of organizing discussion and formulating a policy are enough. They believe that specific policy proposals are necessary. They stick their necks out and make such specific proposals. Few have stuck their necks out further than Magaziner and Reich (1982).

In their book, *Minding American's Business,* Magaziner and Reich (1982) argue that the American economy is losing its competitive position in the international marketplace and is therefore declining. This, they believe, has far-reaching and undesirable consequences. To avoid these, the economy must be redirected by means of a national industrial policy. They provide a detailed analysis of the state of the American economy, documenting the declining standard of living, and they also analyze the deterioration of the steel, color television, and electromechanical industries.

They offer a plan with measures directed at the following objectives:

1. *Easing labor adjustments.* They propose using vouchers to pay for transitional training of workers, requiring advance notification of shutdowns, and providing financial inducements to industries to locate or develop in declining regions.
2. *Correcting market imperfections.* Since private investment may not adequately reflect social interest, government should step in as a "social investor" and make investments with a high social payoff. Following the examples of successful research efforts in Germany, France, and Japan, these investments would include projects in nondefense areas. There would also be policies for supporting such "key linkage industries" as steel, automobile, energy, computer, machine tool, and semiconductor. The health of much of the rest of the economy is assumed to depend on these industries. Social investment, or at least coherent policies, are needed to shore them up.
3. *Encouraging productive investment in long-term projects.* These projects, which would support new products, might otherwise receive insufficient investment because of the weak economy and its uncertain future. Such financial support would include high-risk lending with no obligation to repay unless the effort is successful. Overseas markets for domestic goods would be stimulated, and programs would be installed to support small and medium-sized businesses.
4. *Coordinating government policies.* This repeats the "rationalization" chorus, focusing on government research and development and procurement, capital market policies, trade regulation, and protective measures.

Magaziner may have an opportunity to test his and Reich's

prescriptions. He was the principal author of Rhode Island's "Greenhouse Compact," a piece of legislation that seeks to raise $250 million to finance industrial development in the state. On a per capita basis, this is equivalent to $60 billion at the national level.

Some of the evidence on which Magaziner and Reich's (1982) industrial policy proposals are based is questionable. They argue that the American economy is straining and in danger of collapse. This may be an exaggeration, although the economy is clearly in trouble. Therefore, it is not their conclusions that concern us, but the evidence on which they base them and the implications. They cite the fact that the per capita GNPs of many countries have exceeded that of the United States since the 1970s. It is not apparent to us that having a lower per capita GNP than Switzerland's and Kuwait's is a bad thing or that not being the world's leader in this measure is equivalent to economic decline. If it were the equivalent, it is hard to explain the fact that Switzerland and Kuwait are not mentioned by Magaziner and Reich as world leaders in this or any other connection.

Magaziner and Reich (1982) also cite fewer paid vacations, shorter life expectancies, a higher infant mortality rate, and higher homicide rates in the United States compared with other MDCs as evidence of economic decline. However, these have more to do with quality of life than standard of living. As we noted in the Preface, quality of life and standard of living are not necessarily associated. Either can be improved while the other deteriorates. It is doubtful that a better industrial policy or even increased per capita GNP would have a significant effect on life expectancy, infant mortality, and homicide rates, although it might have some effect on paid vacations.

Throughout their work, Magaziner and Reich (1982) are preoccupied with the alleged decline of investment by the private sector and therefore direct many of their proposals to supplementing investment from public sources. Nationally, the real rates of capital spending increased during the 1970s, with investment in plants leading the way (West and Logue, 1983).

Another objective of Magaziner and Reich's industrial policy is to reduce the vulnerability and decline of America's key linkage industries, of which steel is the most troubled. It does not follow, however, that the problems facing steel, which they consider typical, are also those of the other industries in this category. Robert Lawrence, senior fellow at the Brookings Institution, is reported working on a major study arguing that the erosion of the U.S. industrial base is not significant (Bartlett, 1983, p. 86), the obvious problems of steel notwithstanding. Moreover, it is not at all clear that an industrial policy would increase the long-run viability of steel or of comparable industries, such as shipbuilding. Even in Japan the steel industry is contracting, shutting down excess capacity. Meanwhile, back in the home of industrial policy, Europe, steel is second only to agriculture as a millstone around the EEC's neck.

In countries in which explicitly formulated national industrial policies are already in place, such as most of Europe, it is difficult to identify the economic benefits. Alfred Kahn, who served in the Carter administration, warned: "Cast a skeptical eye on glib references to the alleged success of government interventions in other countries in picking and supporting industrial winners." The successes of these interventions "have been greatly exaggerated" (Bartlett, 1983, p. 86).

Magaziner and Reich (1982) use France, Germany, and Japan as major examples of industrial policy at work. However, the economic prospects of France and Germany are not particularly good. While the German economy is forecast to attain real economic growth of 2% in 1984, in contrast to its 1.1% decline in 1982, the rate of unemployment has climbed from the 1982 figure of 6.9% to over 9% in early 1984.

The situation in France is worse. Real economic growth is forecast to decline from 1.9% in 1982 to 0% in 1984, while unemployment has climbed from 8% to reach 9.5% in early 1984, with more to come. A loss of 100,000 jobs in publicly owned industries and an equal number in the private sector is anticipated. The industrial policy of the Mitterand government is now working well; the government will slash the number of jobs through the spring of 1984 in order to keep inflation and the budget deficit under control. This is robbing Peter to pay Paul. France's steel industry is expected to incur a deficit of $1.2

billion in 1984. Parts of state-owned companies will be sold off to finance the deficit and provide capital for investment in the development of high technology.

Turning to the other side of the world, Philip Trezise of the Brookings Institution has written that Japan's economic success is due less to economic planning than to low taxes and other policies promoting capital formation (Bartlett, 1983, p. 86). The very high savings rate in Japan is due largely to the fact that employers and government offer relatively little to workers after they leave work. Retirement benefits are typically a one-time payment equal to about three years' wages. This creates a strong incentive to save. Fewer managers and better management are also frequently cited as reasons for Japan's success. The argument that this, rather than industrial policy, is responsible for much of Japan's economic growth is supported by the many successful applications of Japanese management principles by American companies.

Few, if any, public policies or programs that have been implemented in the United States in recent years have fulfilled the promises made by the people who had originally proposed them. Even good policies and programs are emasculated when implemented. Can an explicit industrial policy be successfully implemented in the United States? For one thing, it would probably focus on large rather than small enterprises. Although Magaziner and Reich (1982) argue that industrial policy should deal with small and medium-sized businesses, they do not address the implementation problem. Felix Rohatyn is more candid when he states that smaller companies would benefit primarily from what "trickles down" from large companies ("Would Industrial Policy," 1984, p. 72).

This expectation is shared by many others, but some people are not as sanguine about it. John Albertine, head of the American Business Conference, a lobbying group for small businesses, thinks that most small companies would get only the "crumbs" from funds that go to big business: "Those who don't have the political clout will largely be ignored" ("Would Industrial Policy," p. 72). There is evidence to support this view: In 1983 ten exporters received 80 percent of the Export-Import Bank's direct loans.

There are many administrative problems associated with applying an industrial policy that supports small business. The Small Business Administration employs different size criteria for different industries and, according to its chief counsel, spends a great deal of time just "hassling out tough questions such as where you draw the line on size" ("Would Industrial Policy," 1984, p. 72). Administrative costs are higher for small loans than for large ones, eligible companies are harder to identify, and picking the winners is much more difficult.

The widespread concern for small companies is not based on a distaste for bigness but on the important fact that such companies are the principal source of jobs and innovations. Two thirds of the new jobs between 1969 and 1976 were created by firms with no more than twenty employees. Birch (1981, p. 11) asked, "How will [the interventionists] pick out the one out of 100 or 300 firms that will become a major job creator?" In their last report on the economy, President Carter's economic advisors wrote:

> It is presumptuous to assume that successful identifications of winning and losing industrial sectors is possible. . . . Attempts to pick winners or reinvigorate declining industries introduce considerations into strategic industrial decisions that, while not now absent, are certainly less directly felt. Greater government involvement in the detailed workings of the economy has already increased the political aspect of economic decision making and led to constant pressure for the federal government to aid firms, regions, and industries. Establishment of an explicit industrial policy, together with the authorities for implementing it, would intensify these trends [Bartlett, 1983, p. 86].

Our main problem with the well-intentioned proposals of Magaziner and Reich (1982) derives from the fact that they assume economic recovery can take care of unemployment. Consequently, they do not address the migration of labor-intensive industries from MDCs to LDCs, the effect of increased mechanization and automation on employment in industries remaining in MDCs, and the declining percentage of income spent on goods in contrast to services.

We also find little reason to believe that the adoption of industrial policies, however good they may be, can bring about the needed redirection of the economy. The implementation of such policies has always fallen far short of the promises. We think this is due to structural deficiencies in government; therefore, the government must be changed in fundamental ways. We doubt that any reform of government and industry, in contrast to their redesign, can bring about the required redirection of the economy. In Part Two we describe what we think are the major changes required.

Political-Economic Reform

Lester Thurow, in his book *The Zero-Sum Society* (1981), argues that the economic problems of the United States in the 1980s derive from the relationships between energy supplies, growth, and inflation: "Without growing energy supplies, economic growth is difficult, and rapidly rising energy prices provide a powerful inflationary force. Inflation leads to public policies that produce idle capacity and severely retard growth" (p. 191). As a result, he sees the need for deregulation of the energy industry to stimulate competition and promote economic growth. However, he also proposes a number of major changes that are intended both to increase the amount of wealth to be distributed and to make the distribution more equitable.

Thurow (1981) argues that the "invisible hand" can no longer be relied on to guide the economy: "Both politically and intellectually, our history is one of pretending that we can avoid making explicit decisions about the fair distribution of economic resources" (p. 195). Policies covering taxes, expenditures, and regulations must be formulated to promote equity.

Thurow contends that despite widespread verbal commitments to equal opportunity, the economy does not provide it. The ratio of the lowest-paid to the highest-paid fully employed white male is 5:1. But the ratio of the lowest-paid to the highest-paid worker in society as a whole is 27:1. In other words, for

every twenty-seven of the lowest-paid workers in America, there
is one highest-paid worker. The mean earnings of white males in
1977 was $16,568, and $5,843 for all others. Therefore, Thurow
sets as a general equity goal a distribution of earnings over the
whole population that is the same as the current distribution
over fully employed white males.

How can the economy be reorganized so that everyone
can play the same economic game now played by fully employed white males? Thurow proposes changing the structure of
the economy so that it generates enough work of the kind now
available to white males for everyone who wants to work, regardless of age, race, sex, or education. Since private enterprise
would be incapable of providing the required number of jobs, the
federal government would have to make up the shortfall. For a
federal program to succeed, the jobs provided should not be
viewed as temporary, because the lack of job opportunities is a
long-term problem of the economy. In addition, the program
should provide the same opportunities for earnings and promo-
tions that are available to fully employed white males: some
low-wage jobs, some high-wage, and most in the middle. This
would not be a minimum-wage employment program. It should
be open to everyone willing and able to work. Finally, the jobs
provided should be *real* jobs, ones that produce outputs of economic value.

Thurow (1981, p. 206) believes that the principal obstructions to implementing his program are political:

> Politically, we are reluctant to give jobs, be-
> cause to do so would require a major restructuring
> of the economy. A new source of competition
> would arise for both public agencies and private
> firms. To the extent that we are unable or unwill-
> ing to hold the private economy at the full-employ-
> ment level, we would have a socialized economy. . . .
> The only solution is to create a socialized
> sector of the economy designed to give work op-
> portunities to everyone who wants them but can-
> not find them elsewhere.

Realizing that his program would not eliminate the need

for welfare, Thurow (1981) proposes payments that would provide people in need with approximately half of the average per capita standard of living. He also proposes a restructuring of the tax system. He suggests a proportional tax system directed at producing an equitable distribution of after-tax income. Nevertheless, Thurow believes that "taxes are an inferior secondary approach to the problem. They are used only until more fundamental changes can be put in place" (p. 208).

Finally, Thurow (1981) suggests compensating people who would suffer as a consequence of public policies established to promote economic growth. For example, if government support for failing enterprises was greatly reduced, a large number of individuals, investors and workers, would be hurt. Support of their movement to growth industries would be needed. He suggests two possible ways to provide the needed help. The first uses the Japanese model: Large firms would be conglomerated so that resources could be shifted from declining to growing parts of these new companies. The second uses the Swedish model: Extensive social welfare would be provided with substantial resources devoted to retraining. These measures would provide government support of mergers and transitional aid to those adversely affected by them.

Thurow (1981) stresses the fact that economic problems can neither be understood nor solved without taking account of the political process. Our inability to bring about necessary economic changes is largely due to "a political process that cannot make decisions when all decisions result in substantial losses for someone" (p. 212). He argues that the inability to legislate changes that would result in losses to some, even if most would gain, arises from the fact that we do not have political parties:

> A political party is a group that can force its elected members to vote for that party's solution to society's problems. With a majority and minority party, the majority is expected to solve the nation's economic problem. If it can't, it is replaced in the next election, and the minority becomes the majority. Responsibility for success is clear, and failures can be punished [p. 212].

Thurow maintains that in the United States individual candidates, not parties, set the political platforms. There is no longer a clear party responsibility, and no one is inclined to make such unpopular decisions as may be necessary to solve our problems.

This, Thurow (1981) says, is not the case in other MDCs, in which parliamentary forms of government exist and unpopular decisions about the distribution of income can be made: "They can penalize automobile driving, even when everyone drives and loves it. Very high taxes can be levied on gasoline elsewhere, but not here" (p. 212). He concludes:

> There is no easy path for getting from here to there, but somehow we have to establish a political system where someone can be held responsible for failure. This can only be done in a system where there are disciplined majority and minority parties. Every politician with his or her own platform is the American way, but it is not a way that is going to be able to solve America's economic problems [p. 214].

We are very sympathetic with Thurow's (1981) objectives of economic equity and political equality. We agree with his diagnosis of the principal obstruction to their attainment: measures perceived as involving losses by some, usually those who benefit most from the current state of affairs. These beneficiaries of the status quo are able to block such measures. As Thurow says, our society is engaged in a zero-sum game in which one party's gain is invariably perceived as another's equivalent loss. This win-lose view of social interactions results in adversarial bargaining that paralyzes our society.

Thurow (1981) addresses the unemployment problem head-on, recognizing that some of the measures required to revitalize the economy are likely to exacerbate the problem. He proposes to handle it by massive government employment. Aware of the poor record of government in creating "real" jobs, he specifies that the jobs created have output of economic value. But he does not suggest how this can be accomplished. In view of our government's very poor record in this regard, why should we believe that it might now create jobs that create rather than consume wealth? We do not mean to imply that this cannot be done, only that it seems very unlikely unless government is changed more radically than Thurow suggests.

Thurow's (1981) proposed corrective measures involve more interventions by a centralized government whose role in society would thereby be increased. Big government would become much bigger. Although he acknowledges the current inefficiency and ineffectiveness of government, he does not fret over the possibility that making government bigger would exacerbate these problems. The record gives us reason to believe that there are diseconomies of government's scale. The most intervening governments in the world, and relatively the largest, have not produced the most vigorous economies.

Are the only alternatives bigger centralized government and a larger role for the invisible hand? We think not. In Part Two we suggest ways of revitalizing the economy and producing the number and kinds of jobs required that involve decreasing the size of central government by decentralizing and dispersing it.

Most of Thurow's (1981) proposals involve reforms—changes of behavior of the current system—rather than fundamental restructuring of it. The most radical structural change he suggests is to a parliamentary form of government. Although we agree with his perception that our system has difficulty in making hard decisions, we are not convinced that a parliamentary system will do better, even if it can do better. Consider those European countries that already have such governments. Have they shown a greater ability than ours to deal effectively with their economic problems? Parliamentary government, even if necessary, is clearly not sufficient to take us on the hard path from here to there. To be sure, Margaret Thatcher is able to make less popular decisions than is the president of the United States, but her hard decisions do not appear to be any more effective than a president's "easy" ones. It seems to us that there must be a way to make tough decisions that are likelier to succeed than those that have been made in Europe. We believe that the solution lies not so much in how centralized decision makers are organized, as in who should make the decisions and how they should be made. We also address these questions in Part Two.

Radical Transformation

Some people believe that the economies of Western MDCs cannot be revitalized without a thorough overhaul of their socioeconomic systems; reform will not do. Hazel Henderson is among the most prominent of these proponents of radical change.

In her book *Creating Alternative Futures: The End of Economics* (1978) and in many other publications, Henderson argues that what is needed most to reinvigorate our societies and their economies is a change of paradigm, a new perspective, a different way of viewing the world. Policies derived from the old and outworn paradigm cannot do the job. A new paradigm is emerging but is not widely recognized and therefore is not being used to maximum advantage. She sees economists as the principal obstruction to awareness and understanding by government and the public of the fundamental changes that are taking place.

Henderson (1978) argues that economic systems, like their biological counterparts, eventually reach a point at which they stop growing. At this point growth gives way to differentiation and maintenance. Competition for previously abundant resources is replaced by cooperation in the use of those that are scarce, and exploitation of the ecosystem converts into its restoration and preservation.

Henderson (1978) claims that these changes are now taking place throughout the world at an accelerating rate. During this transitional process, severe stresses and strains are felt by nations, regions, corporations, communities, and individuals. Many of these either ignore the changes or attempt to explain them away by use of the old paradigm, thus minimizing their impact. According to Henderson, individuals and all their collectivities should be trying to adapt to these changes. Such adaptation that is now taking place is occurring only at the lower levels of society. Therefore, it is at the lower levels that solutions to our social problems should be sought, found, and implemented. For example, it is at the grass-roots level that a "countereconomy" and "counterculture" are being created:

> Far from being faddish, the counter-culture and citizen protest movements of the past decade that are forming the nucleus of the emerging counter-economies based on self-reliant, decentralized, ecologically harmonious lifestyles, are deadly serious and must be explicitly documented and reinforced, since they represent the best repositories of social and cultural flexibility during the decline now underway in many mature industrial countries and the coming contraction in its system of world trade [Henderson, pp. 384-385].

Individuals are demanding more and more control over their lives. Many of the grass-roots movements of the 1960s and 1970s have become national causes that promote the values of a cooperative and ecologically sound society that has moved beyond the imperative of growth. These include the environmentalist, consumerist, and women's rights movements. Some people are beginning to realize that technology is not the panacea that many still think it is. It has as much potential for creating problems as for solving them. For this reason, Henderson (1978) sees a greater role for the public in assessing proposed and current technology.

She argues that hierarchical bureaucracies should be replaced by decentralized, participative networks that foster social innovation and adaptation. The effective use of mass media greatly facilitates the transition required. They can promote awareness and understanding of the crises and problems that abound. Moreover, they can be used to provide instant two-way public communication, thereby making possible participative democracy on a national scale.

Henderson (1978) believes that the new culture and economy that are emerging have shifted the focus from the acquisition of material possessions, "Jonesism," to improvement of the quality of life. She uses a Harris survey taken in May 1977 to confirm this value shift:

It found that by 79% to 17%, the public
would place greater emphasis on teaching people
how to live more with basic essentials "than on
reaching a higher standard of living." By 76% to
17%, a sizable majority opts for "learning to get
our pleasures out of nonmaterial experiences" rather than on "satisfying our needs for more goods
and services." . . . By 63% to 29%, a majority feels
that the country would be better served if emphasis were put on "learning how to appreciate human
values more than material values," rather than on
"finding ways to produce more jobs for producing
more goods" [p. 395].

Among the proposals Henderson (1978) makes for government are the following: extended unemployment benefits;
a major conservation plan involving national control of domestic energy resources; mandatory fuel allocation and rationing;
policies to foster a shift to a low-capital-investment, highly
labor-intensive economy; bank reform; requirement of "Employment Impact Statements" (modeled on Environmental Impact Statements) for major investments; stronger antitrust measures; control of advertising to make it informational; spreading
stock ownership through employee stock-option plans; and major changes in the tax code to replace tax credits for investment
in general by credit allocations based on the social desirability
of the investment. She also proposes federally funded programs
for public service employment and the rapid implementation of
federal programs now authorized for rebuilding America's infrastructure primarily through federal jobs.

We agree with Henderson (1978) that the prevailing view
of the world is changing and that awareness and understanding
of this change open possibilities for redirecting our affairs more
effectively than would otherwise be apparent to us. We also
agree with Henderson that growth should no longer be accepted
by a society as an end in itself. However, we think that basing
this belief on a biological analogy can be misleading. Society
and social groups are not organisms. Unlike organisms, their
parts have purposes of their own. Henderson is obviously aware
of this, but we think that she does not take advantage of some
of its implications. We do not see growth as either necessarily

evil or necessarily limited. It is a means, not an end, and is therefore an option that should be evaluated relative to explicitly formulated societal objectives. We take *development* to be the end that purposeful individuals and groups should seek. Development, as we conceive it, is not a biological but a psychological and social concept. It is with respect to their potential contribution to development that proposals for revitalizing societies and their economies should be evaluated.

Henderson argues for the need to decentralize power. Nevertheless, she proposes major federal programs to create jobs, control advertising, and allocate national fuel resources, among other things. She leaves vague the method of implementing these programs, but their mere existence would seem to contradict her desire to disperse power. National programs that are centrally administered would be susceptible to the same political pressures that now produce resistance to change and, when such resistance is overcome, dilute and distort the programs that are implemented.

Nevertheless, as will be seen, there are many elements of Henderson's (1978) work that we absorb in ours—for example, the need to decentralize government, greater participation in public affairs, and less formal organizational arrangements. She has made a very large number of specific proposals, but they are not brought together into a cohesive and unified design. This does not mean that they are internally inconsistent but that they are difficult to grasp as a whole. The role, relevance, and interactions of her proposals are not always apparent to us.

On the other hand, it is apparent that the sequence of proposals we have reviewed in this chapter move progressively from simplicity to complexity. These proposals differ not only in content and complexity, but in kind: They are based on different implicit concepts of ways to treat a problem.

Some Reflections on Ways to Treat a Problem

A problem is a situation that satisfies three conditions: First, a decision maker (individual or group) has several courses of action available; second, the choice can have a significant effect, one that makes a difference to the decision maker; third, the decision maker has some doubt about which choice to make. Consequently, there are four ways in which problems can be treated: *absolving, resolving, solving,* and *dissolving.*

Problem Absolving. Problem absolvers try to ignore problems in the hope or expectation that they will go away or be taken care of in the natural course of events. They believe that interventions are likelier to intensify and extend the duration of problems than leaving the problems alone. Problem absolvers resist the temptation to act until their survival or stability is threatened—until there is a crisis. Therefore, they practice what is known as crisis management. Crisis managers do as little as possible to remove crises; they do not address the problems from which the crises arise. These people are clearly conservative and inactive; they resist and try to prevent change in an effort to maintain things as they are. Although they do not usually claim that things are as good as possible, they believe that things are as good as we have reason or right to expect.

Problem Resolving. Problem resolvers try to select a course of action that yields an outcome that is good enough, that "satisfices" (satisfies and suffices). Their approach to problems is clinical: They treat each problem as unique and rely heavily on past experience and trial and error in treating problems. Problem resolving is qualitatively, not quantitatively, oriented. It makes extensive use of subjective judgments and common sense. Problem resolvers occasionally make use of research, even quantitative research, but they seldom use it exclusively or allow it to play a decisive role.

Problem resolvers attempt to reconstruct a previous state in which the problem they are facing did not exist. They look for the cause of a problem, what is to blame for it, and try to remove or neutralize the cause so that things can go back to how they once were. Because they react to problems and try to treat them by returning to a previous state, they are *reactionary.*

Most decision makers in government and private enterprise are problem resolvers. They defend this approach by citing the lack of time and information that other approaches require.

They also argue that real problems are so messy as to render more sophisticated approaches infeasible. Furthermore, they claim their experiential approach to problems minimizes the risk of making a serious error of commission, doing what should not be done. They are less concerned with errors of omission, not doing what should be done.

Problem Solving. Problem solvers try to do as well as possible, to optimize. They are research oriented, making heavy use of scientific method, techniques, and tools. They are disposed to quantitative procedures, experimentation, observation, and measurement. They denigrate the subjectivity of the clinical approach and aspire to complete objectivity.

Those who try to solve problems tend to be liberals, seeking to reform the system that has the problem so as to take advantage of changes that are inevitable. They try to do so by predicting change, preparing for it, and accelerating it when possible. They are "preactive," seeking to exploit changes that cannot be avoided, and they focus on minimizing errors of omission, or lost opportunities.

This approach to problems is favored by technologically oriented managers and management scientists, whose organizational objective is not survival, as it is for problem absolvers, or revival, as it is for problem resolvers, but growth.

Problem Dissolving. Problem dissolvers try to change a system so as to remove the problem. They idealize rather than satisfice or optimize; that is, their objective is to move the system involved closer to its ultimately desired state, its ideal. They take a design approach to problems, redesigning the system involved so that it can control as much of its future as possible and respond rapidly and effectively to those changes that it cannot control. Problem dissolvers try to help those who have a problem to do better in the future than the best that can be done now. They do this by designing their currently most desired future and inventing or finding ways of approximating it as closely as possible.

Problem dissolvers are interactive; they change how systems interact with their environments and how their parts interact with each other. Both the system's structure and its functioning are changed. These changes are radical, directed toward development, not growth.

Classifying the Theorists Reviewed. It is clear, we hope, that people who believe that an inevitable economic recovery will solve the unemployment problem absolve themselves of the problem. However, to suggest, as some do, that others deal with the problem—for example, a national commission, council, or committee—is not to let affairs take their own course; it is personal absolution of the problem. It is more than personal when people who suggest that others discuss the problem realize that their chances of solving it are minimal. Most people who suggest such dialogue must be aware of the impotence of the proposed groups.

Advocates of national industrial policy as a solution to our economic problems seem to us to be problem resolving. They identify deficiencies in the current situation and propose corrective (reactive) measures. The intended outcome of their proposals seems to be a return to the economic conditions of the good old days, the 1960s. This they obviously consider to be good enough.

Thurow (1981) goes beyond this. He seeks something we have never had, economic equity and political equality. Therefore, he tries to solve the unemployment problem. He tries to create a better state of affairs than we have ever had by doing what he considers to be the best that can be done. He focuses on what can be done now to improve the future, but not on increasing our future ability and desire to improve the future. Except for his proposal for a parliamentary form of government, his proposals are for reform through more government interventions, but not ones that are radically different from those of the past. The differences are more of degree than of kind.

Henderson (1978) does propose radical changes in the nature and structure of government and society. Her approach seems to us to approximate that of designing. She tries to dissolve the unemployment problem by creating a society in which there could be no involuntary unemployment. However, as we observed, her design is neither cohesive nor directed at an explicitly formulated objective.

In all the proposals we have reviewed in this chapter except Henderson's (1978), the growth of the economy is the principal objective. Therefore, they focus on the standard of living. Those who advocate a national industrial policy are primarily concerned with the average standard of living; Thurow (1981) is more concerned with its distribution. Henderson rejects growth and the economists' concept of standard of living, but she does not explicitly formulate her own objective. We think she is more concerned with improving the quality of life and its distribution than doing this for the standard of living. If this is correct, then her objective is development rather than growth.

Because the difference between adopting growth and adopting development as an objective is profound, we shall explore their difference.

Growth Versus Development. Growth, strictly speaking, is an increase in size or number. Organisms can increase in size, and populations can increase in number. Economic growth, therefore, refers either to an increase in the size of an economy (for example, its GNP) or an increase in a measure of its performance (for example, per capita income).

Growth usually occurs without choice in most biological systems. In human beings, however, choices can deter or accelerate it as, for example, in the choice of diet. If an otherwise normal human being has a compulsion to grow physically, he or she is likely to be considered mentally ill. However, we consider a society's compulsion to grow as being natural, even laudable. Why? Because we assume that physical or economic growth is necessary, if not sufficient, for development. This is not a correct assumption. Nevertheless, if limits to growth limited development, one could understand a preoccupation with growth. Not even the authors of *The Limits to Growth* (Meadows and others, 1972) say that this is the case.

Development of a person or a society, contrary to what many believe, is not a condition or state defined by what or how much that person or society has. For example, if the goods and services available in the most affluent nation were suddenly made available to an underdeveloped country, that nation would not thereby become developed. Development has less to do with how much a person or society has than with what it can do with whatever it has. For this reason, Robinson Crusoe and the Swiss Family Robinson are better paradigms of development than John D. Rockefeller or J. P. Morgan.

Development is a process in which individuals or societies increase their abilities and desires to satisfy their own needs and desires and those of others. It is much more a matter of learning than of earning. It is better reflected in quality of life than in standard of living. It has become increasingly apparent that the continued economic growth of a nation is not necessarily accompanied by improvements in the quality of life. Many argue, as Henderson (1978) does, that some of the most economically advanced countries are now increasing their standards of living at the expense of quality of life.

This is not to say that wealth is irrelevant to development or the quality of life; it is very relevant. How much people can actually improve their quality of life and that of others depends not only on the people's abilities and desires but also on what resources are available to them. However, it should be kept in mind that resources are more often taken from nature than given by it. The more developed a country or person, the more resources it has to recognize and develop. The more dependent one is on the resources that are handed over, the less developed that individual is. Put another way, resources are created by what nature provides. What nature provides is not a resource until people have transformed it or learned how to use it.

Because development involves an increase of ability and desire, and because one person or society cannot learn or be motivated for another, *one person or society cannot develop another.* One can only encourage and facilitate the development of another. There is only one type of development: *self-development.* Therefore, governments cannot develop the governed, but they can encourage and facilitate the development of the governed. Therefore, if we view unemployment as a problem whose dissolution is an opportunity for development rather than growth, we look not for what governments can do to solve the problem, but for what they can do to encourage and facilitate solution of the problem by the governed.

Conclusion

The proposals we develop in Part Two are directed at society's development, not its economic growth, but we do not preclude the possibility or even the desirability of such growth. We view the reduction of unemployment more as a way of improving the quality of life than of increasing the standard of living. Our effort to deal with the problem is a dissolving effort. We try to redesign society so as to make the problem disappear. Our design is not one of a society that can easily be realized, but one that is idealized. Idealized designs are not attainable, but they can be approached without limit. More important, when people confront such a design, they generally find that it can be approximated much more closely than they had believed beforehand. When they contemplate their own idealized designs, they cannot avoid recognizing that the principal obstruction between them and where they most want to be is *themselves*. Pogo put it beautifully when he said: "We have met the enemy and they is us." We deal with feasibility not when designing but afterwards. We believe that working backward from where we want to be to an attainable state yields a more advanced state than working forward from where we are.

A design consists of a *system* of decisions. This means that it has properties that none of its parts do, and its parts acquire properties from the design that they would not otherwise have. Therefore, it is possible to have a feasible design none of which elements, considered separately, are feasible.

Before we turn to what ought to and can be done to dissolve the unemployment problem, we shall reexamine the problem of unemployment and reformulate it in light of the discussion up to this point.

4

Reformulating
the Problem

In Chapter One we showed why the work force in MDCs is expected to increase significantly over at least the rest of this century. First, the number of people of working age will increase because of the number already born and expected to survive. Second, an increasing percentage of women are likely to enter the labor force. Third, if life expectancy continues to increase and morbidity to decrease, a diminishing percentage of people will leave the work force because of death or illness.

Where can the required number of additional jobs come from? They are not likely to come from production industries, because the percentage of the work force employed in these industries has been declining, and this decline appears likely to continue for three reasons. First, labor-intensive industries in MDCs will probably continue to migrate to LDCs, where labor is cheaper. Second, those industries that remain in MDCs are expected to automate more in order to stay competitive in the international marketplace, and this will decrease the number of employees. Third, the demand for goods in MDCs is no longer increasing as rapidly as it once did. On the other hand, the demand for goods in LDCs might increase. Although most LDCs prefer to develop their own production capabilities, it will be some time before they will be able to meet all their internal demand, particularly for capital goods. However, even if the demand for goods from LDCs increases, it appears unlikely that production industries in MDCs will increase their employment enough to absorb future increases in the labor force, let alone the currently unemployed.

These trends suggest increasing unemployment. To prevent this, new jobs must be created. If they are unlikely to come from production industries, can they come from service? Although current trends indicate an increasing desire for services, this desire may not be translated into demand unless government and industry make some significant changes in how they provide these services. Before discussing what changes are required and why, we shall consider why the desire for services is likely to increase.

Desire for Services

The strongest reason for believing that the desire for services in MDCs will increase is the growing preoccupation with quality of life. This quality of life, in contrast to the standard of living, is more a matter of aesthetics than economics. First, it involves the satisfaction we derive from what we do, regardless of why we do it. This reflects an activity's *intrinsic* value. For example, the satisfaction we derive from a walk through the country, reading, visiting a museum, or watching a movie contributes to our quality of life. The quality of *work* life depends on the amount of enjoyment extracted from it. Such satisfaction, pleasure, and enjoyment are *recreative* in nature. Recreation, especially play, is an activity whose value is almost entirely intrinsic, engaged in for its own sake, for the fun of it. To the extent that work or learning is fun, it has intrinsic value and contributes to our quality of life.

Second, quality of life involves the satisfaction we derive from the effects of what we do. These effects reflect *extrinsic* value. For example, our quality of life is increased by the satisfaction we derive from learning something that enables us to do what we want to do, from making something useful or attractive, or from contributing to something we consider worthwhile. Therefore, quality of life also depends on the meaningfulness of what we do, the significance and value of its consequences. Put another way, the extrinsic value of what we do is the progress we make by doing it. Progress is *creative* rather than recreative. To the extent that work, play, or learning involves creative activity, it has extrinsic value and contributes to our development and quality of life.

Our quality of life obviously depends on our ability to use the resources available. For example, it may be fun driving an automobile to a place but not walking there. However, if we do not know how to drive, the availability of an automobile will not be a source of satisfaction. Some people can extract a great deal of pleasure from very little; others are not able to extract any satisfaction from a great deal. Quality of life depends more on what we do with what we have than on what we have. It depends more on the services we can either provide ourselves or obtain from others than on the amount of goods we have. For this reason, as people become more concerned with quality of life than with standard of living, their desire for service, including self-service, becomes greater than their desire for material possessions.

Potential Employment in Services

All services are not desired equally, and all do not require equal amounts of labor. Therefore, different services have different potential for creating jobs. Table 5 gives information on those services in which employment is growing at least as rapidly as the economy of the United States; it also gives information on the production industries. In 1981, 54 percent of the work force was engaged in services in which employment was increasing more rapidly than it was in production industries.

Let us consider a few of these service categories in more detail.

Health. Life expectancy is increasing in the MDCs of the West as well as in the world (Table 6). Despite increasing life expectancies, population growth rates are declining in North America and Europe because of restrictive immigration laws and declining birth rates (Table 7).

U.S. Medicare and Medicaid payments for the aged in-

Table 5. Employment Growth Rates in Selected Industries.

Economic Sector	Percent Increase in Employment 1970-1981	Percent Total Employed in 1981
Service industries	142	54
Business services	179	3
Entertainment and recreation	154	1
Finance, insurance, and real estate	155	6
Health services	214	3
Hospitals	147	4
Schools, colleges, and universities	124	8
Transportation, communication, and other public utilities	125	7
Welfare and religious agencies	197	2
Wholesale and retail trade	137	20
Production industries[a]	111	29
Total	126	100

[a]Mining, construction, and manufacturing.
Source: Bureau of the Census, 1982, table 652.

Table 6. World Life Expectancy.

Area	1960	1980	1985 (Projected)
More Developed Regions			
Male	66.3	69.0	69.5
Female	72.5	75.4	75.8
North America			
Male	66.9	68.5	68.8
Female	73.5	75.7	75.8
Europe			
Male	67.0	69.8	70.4
Female	72.3	75.4	75.9
World			
Male	50.9	57.9	59.2
Female	53.5	60.5	62.2

Source: Bureau of the Census, 1982, tables 856, 861, and 862.

Table 7. Annual Growth Rates of Population, 1950-1979.

Regions	1950-1955	1955-1960	1960-1965	1965-1970	1970-1975	1975-1979
More Developed	1.3%	1.3%	1.2%	0.9%	0.8%	0.7%
Less Developed	2.1	2.3	2.2	2.6	2.4	2.1

Source: Bureau of the Census, 1980b, table 2.

creased from $9.4 billion in 1971 to $94.2 billion in 1982. Expenditures on health have been increasing much faster than the rate of inflation (Table 8). With more older people (Table 9) and more effective treatments of diseases and disabilities, the demand for health services is likely to continue to increase.

In 1975, 4,100,000 people were employed in major health occupations. This increased by 25 percent to 5,140,000 in 1980, and an additional 4 percent to 5,338,000 in 1981. Clearly, there is reason to believe that the desire for health services will increase and that this field will provide increased employment opportunities.

Table 8. Percent Changes from Previous Year in Expenditures on Health, Total Expenditures, and the Consumer Price Index, 1965-1981.

Category	1965	1970	1975	1980	1981
Percent Change in Per Capita Health Expenditure	8.2	8.8	11.4	16.1	12.9
(Total Per Capita Expenditure)	($144)	($207)	($325)	($ 586)	($ 662)
Percent Change in Total National Expenditure	7.1	11.1	11.0	14.5	14.0
(Total Expenditure in Billions)	($193)	($332)	($565)	($1,024)	($1,167)
Percent Change in Consumer Price Index	1.3	4.3	6.9	9.0	10.4

Source: Bureau of the Census, 1982, tables 152 and 754.

Table 9. U.S. Population 65 Years of Age and Over.

Year	Number (thousands)	Percent Total Population
1920	4,586	4.8
1940	8,385	7.1
1960	15,304	9.6
1978	21,800	11.5
2000 (Projected)	28,155	12.9

Source: Bureau of the Census, 1980a, table 1/5.

Education. Expenditures for education have been increasing in both relative and absolute terms. In the United States, for example, expenditures (in current dollars) for public and private schools increased 7.34 times from 1960 to 1981, 1.26 times as much as the GNP. The portion of the GNP spent on public and private schools rose from 4.9 percent in 1960 to 7.3 percent in 1970, but declined to 6.5 percent in 1981 because of a decline in enrollment. Expenditures (in constant 1980 dollars) per pupil in daily attendance in public elementary and secondary schools rose from $1,247 in 1960, to $1,963 in 1970, to $2,494 in 1980. Most striking is the fact that government expenditures on all types as education increased by a factor of 21.7 from 1960 to 1979. In addition, "the [U.S.] public appears to be committed to the expenditure of money to improve the Nation's education system. A continuing survey conducted by the National Opinion Research Center indicated that only 1 of 10 respondents believed too much was being spent on education and half or more indicated they believed too little was being spent to improve education" (Bureau of the Census, 1980a, p. 254).

The United States is by no means the largest spender on education. In 1975 U.S. expenditures on education were 6.2 percent of the GNP, but 7.9 percent in Canada, 8.3 percent in Denmark, 7.9 percent in the Netherlands (1973), 7.1 percent in Norway, and 7.5 percent in Sweden (1974).

Although the U.S. National Center for Education Statistics projects no significant change in the number of students enrolled in primary and secondary public and private schools—

from 58.25 million in 1979 to 58.04 million in 1989—it projects a 5 percent increase in college enrollment, from 11.57 million in 1979 to 12.14 million in 1989. Between 1960 and 1980 total enrollment in higher education in the United States increased 3.2 times. Related expenditures increased 4.5 times between 1965 and 1979. The increasing employment of those in jobs that require higher levels of formal training is clearly shown in Table 10.

Table 10. Change in Numbers of Workers by Occupation
Between 1972 and 1981.

Occupation	Percent Change
Managers and administrators, nonfarm	43
Professional, technical, and related workers	42
Clerical and related workers	30
Service workers except private household	29
Sales workers	19
Craft and related workers	17
Transport equipment operatives	8
Laborers, nonfarm	8
Operatives, nontransport	1
Farm laborers and supervisors	−9
Farmers and farm managers	−14
Private household workers	−29

Source: Bureau of the Census, 1982, table 651.

Although the number employed by government in education decreased between 1975 and 1980, the percentage of government employees working in education increased from 18 to 20. The number of additional teachers required in public elementary and secondary schools estimated by the U.S. Department of Education is 670,000 between 1981 and 1985 and 983,000 between 1986 and 1990.

If the rate of technological change increases as expected, there will be more demand for continuing education. The amount of time spent by corporate and government employees in such education has been increasing rapidly, and this increase is likely to continue. In addition, the increasing demand for professional and managerial workers that is expected will also increase the need for some college education: "The rapid change ahead . . . means that you cannot expect to remain in the same job or profession for life. . . . The coming changes will force us to seek retraining again and again. Business will have to play the key role, similar to the way IBM now spends approximately $500 million annually on employee training and education" (Naisbitt, 1982, p. 37). Unfortunately, reliable data on the amount being spent by corporations on education are not available. Estimates vary between $4 billion and $100 billion per year. The consensus seems to be that the figure is around $30 billion and growing rapidly.

On the other hand, the widely proclaimed and documented decline of the quality of public education could lead to a reduction in expenditures on education, but this decline is likelier to produce demands for improvements that will increase expenditures:

> Many new jobs could . . . be created in the schools if we took the giant, but very expensive step of really reducing class-size. Think how many more children could learn, and teachers could teach, in classes of 10-15 students per teacher, like those now available in the private schools to which the rich send their children. And how about children's libraries in every neighborhood, staffed by people who can help the children with their homework when parents cannot do so [Gans, 1977, p. 44]?

The recommendations made in the widely publicized report on public education by the National Commission on Excellence in Education (1983) would also require increased expenditures.

Communication. Between 1960 and 1981, the U.S. GNP increased 2.3 times in constant 1972 dollars. In the same period, the GNP in communications increased 4.7 times, more than twice as much. Since 1975, both total national employment and employment in the communications industry has increased by about 17 percent.

The most dramatic recent changes in communications

have occurred in cable television and electronic mail. In 1950 there were 70 cable television systems in the United States; in 1982 there were 4,825—sixty-nine times as many. In 1950 there were about 10,000 subscribers; in 1982, there were 21 million. The introduction of direct satellite-to-house TV transmission will undoubtedly increase this number significantly.

A major prospect for growth in communications lies in electronic mail. Future Systems Incorporated has estimated that by the year 2000, 80 percent of conventional business-to-business private mail will be electronic, 50 percent of business-to-business first-class mail, and 20 percent of business-to-home and home-to-business mail. In addition, facsimile communications equipment sold in 1973 was valued at $11.8 million and $123.6 million in 1980. Future Systems Incorporated predicts the figure will increase to about $2 billion by 2000.

New types of communications equipment and services are announced almost daily; for example, a portable wireless telephone about the size of a cigarette pack has been introduced. Telephones will be made available in all intercity conveyances. Video communication is still in its infancy, but major applications of it are expected soon. The proliferation of home computers is making a new type of communication available to households, such as the transmission of information, orders, and bills. Clearly, employment in producing new communications equipment and providing communications services can be expected to increase.

The continuing dispersion of corporate activities and greater mobility of the work force will also create a greater need for communication. More leisure time will increase the use of entertainment communicated to the home. More educational uses of communications media can also be expected. The use of radio and television by the Open University in the United Kingdom foreshadows this development.

Travel. The U.S. population increased by 52 percent from 1947 to 1978. In the same period, the number of intercity passenger miles traveled increased by 261 percent. Total U.S. employment increased by 126 percent from 1970 to 1981. In the same period, the number of employees in auto services increased

by 65 percent, in airlines by 29 percent, and in transport services by 84 percent.

The increased mobility of the work force, the extension
of corporate markets, and the dispersion of corporate as well as
governmental operations will also increase the need for travel (in
addition to the need for communications). Contrary to popular
belief, increased communication does not decrease the demand
for travel. The availability of the telephone did not decrease
travel; it increased it. Because of the telephone, people could
communicate with people who were increasingly dispersed. This
created a need and a desire for face-to-face contact with these
people and hence more travel. Moreover, cinema and television
have increased the desire for travel as recreation. Seeing an attractive place on television is no more a substitute for visiting
it than seeing a TV commercial for food is a substitute for eat-
ing that food. Between 1960 and 1977, overseas travel from the
United States increased by 450 percent, and there is every
reason to expect continuing increases in travel.

Leisure and Recreation. The average number of leisure
hours per week for city dwellers in the United States increased
from 34.8 in 1965 to 38.5 in 1975, an 11 percent increase. The
largest portion of this time was spent watching television, which
increased from 10.4 hours per week in 1965 to 15.2 hours in
1975, a 46 percent increase. From 1950 to 1977, national income derived from motion pictures and amusement and recreation services increased by 559 percent. In addition, personal
expenditures for leisure and cultural activities increased from
$17.9 billion in 1960 to $91.2 billion in 1978, an increase of
411 percent. As a portion of the GNP, these expenditures rose
from 3.5 to 4.3 percent over the same period. Also, the development of portable radios, television sets, and tape recorders has increased the amount of time listening to or watching
them.

With decreasing time spent at work and longer retire-
ments, more time is likely to be spent in leisure and recreational
activity. Therefore, recreational services can be expected to
grow even more than in the past.

Social Services. U.S. per capita expenditures (in constant

1977 dollars) for social welfare increased 4.33 times between 1950 and 1977. In the same period, the GNP increased only 3.78 times. Increases in the number of retirees and older persons will place more demands on social services. As a result of the dissolution of the extended family, an increasing number of older people are living alone. Their requirements for public assistance are greater than those of older people living with their children.

The rapid growth of one-parent families is also likely to create new demands for social services. In 1970 there were 398,700 out-of-wedlock births in the United States. This increased to 686,605 by 1981. In 1950 only 4 percent of the children born in the United States were born outside marriages. This figure rose to 10.7 percent in 1970 and 18.9 percent in 1981.

Another new social phenomenon, the rapidly increasing underclass (discussed in Chapter One), is also likely to increase requirements for social services.

In addition, growing public concern for the welfare of the disabled, handicapped, and disadvantaged is likely to increase the demand for social services. The concept of the "undeserving poor" seems to be disappearing. As a result, the elimination of poverty is likely to become an increasingly important social objective.

In sum, the need for social services appears certain to increase. How much of this need will be met obviously depends on political decisions, which will reflect both cost and public opinion. Despite short-term fluctuations, the public in most MDCs has favored more, not less, public assistance. The number of people who could be employed in providing such assistance is very large indeed.

Maintenance and Improvement of the Environment. Although this category of service is not used in our national accounts, information relating to it can be extracted from census data. Federal expenditures (in constant 1978 dollars) devoted to improving and protecting the environment increased from $5.4 billion in 1973 to $11.0 billion in 1978, a 103 percent increase. In this same period, the GNP (also in constant dollars) increased by only 63 percent. The number of civilians employed by the U.S. government in environmental protection increased by 15 percent from 1975 to 1978. In this same period, total civilian employment by the government decreased by 2 percent.

The infrastructure of many cities is old and in serious disrepair. This reduces the quality of urban living. The conditions of streets, expressways, bridges, public transport, utility delivery systems, solid waste collection and disposal, street cleaning, litter, and graffiti pose only a few of the many problems. Upgrading urban facilities and services could productively employ very large numbers of people. However, doing so is costly. If the repairs, maintenance, and services were less expensive, the public, we believe, would be willing to support much more of them. We later consider how these costs might be reduced.

The Roots of the Unemployment Problem

We have tried to show that the desire for a variety of services will probably continue to increase. Therefore, under the right conditions, people could be employed to provide these services. This would significantly reduce unemployment, but we believe that significant changes must first be made in how services are provided. This belief is based on the current high cost and low quality of many services. Many people who need or want these services feel that they are not worth their cost. Whatever service we purchase, for ourselves or others, has some value to us, but so does what we pay for it. If the value of the service we receive is less than the value we give up to obtain it, our wealth is reduced. The acquisition of many services is widely perceived as wealth decreasing rather than wealth increasing. Two examples of this are public education and health care. As long as services are perceived in this way, much of the growing need and desire for them will go unfulfilled and, therefore, not yield the number of jobs required to reduce unemployment significantly.

The low value-to-cost ratio associated with many services derives from the fact that they are provided by bureaucratic monopolies either within the government or in the private sector. Private monopolies are usually regulated and protected against competition by government. Utilities are the most conspicuous examples.

Why do public and private bureaucratic monopolies so often provide services whose cost exceeds their value? The answer to this question lies in the nature of monopolies and bureaucracies and why they often go together.

Monopoly. An organization is a monopoly if it has exclusive control of or a right to control some commodity or service. Many government service agencies are monopolies. As E. S. Savas (1982, p. 20) noted: "Lacking competitors, a monopoly agency is inexorably driven to exercise its power and exploit its monolithically secure position." B. D. Henderson (1982) elaborated upon this allegation: "The unlimited power of government overrides the constraints of cost, value, efficiency and productivity imposed by the marketplace. Consequently, the services provided by a government tend to be far more costly than those subject to the freedom and natural selectivity of the marketplace" (p. 11).

S. H. Hanke (1984) provides some recent evidence to support these charges:

> Item: Scottsdale, Ariz., saves $2 million a year by contracting for fire protection.
> Item: One third of the refuse in Newark, N.J., is privately collected, saving $200,000 a year.
> Item: Dallas closed its municipal late-night gasoline depots; now police cars and some fire vehicles use gas pumps at 7-11 stores after midnight, saving $200,000 annually.
> Item: A private firm operates the Orange County, Calif., computer center, at an annual savings of $1.6 million.
> Item: Butte, Mont., contracted for the private operation of its municipal hospital; annual savings are $600,000.
> Item: Newton, Mass., saves $500,000 a year through a contract with a firm that supplies the city with paramedical and ambulance service.

Private monopolies fare no better. According to Hazel

Henderson (1978, p. 124): "Citizens now wonder if they [oli-gopolies] can be relied upon to deliver uninterrupted electricity and all the consumer durables on which we have become hooked, with adequate safety and reliability, at prices we can afford and with tolerable levels of pollution and disruption of other community values." The apparent lack of concern with public safety in the construction and operation of atomic energy plants has seriously undermined the public's faith in monopolistic utilities and government's ability to regulate them effectively. Oligopoly, market control in the hands of a few pro-viders, is not much better:

> They [oligopolies] all must administer prices because they have similar problems and advantages. Their flexibility is limited by the very bigness of their projects and sales and by the long lead time required to put their products on the markets. They all face similar wage demands. . . . If one were to lower its prices, the others would follow and none would gain. If one raised its prices ahead of the others, its share of the market would fall dramatically. . . . Administered pricing is a logical consequence [Muller, 1980, pp. 61–62].

Monopolies and oligopolies, whether public or private, are not motivated to provide goods and services at a price ap-propriate to their value to consumers. They do not have to com-pete for consumer purchases or subsidies. Moreover, they tend to bureaucratize, which adds to their costs, precisely because they do not have to compete in order to survive.

Bureaucracy. A bureaucracy is an organization that is de-signed to operate as much like a machine as possible because its designers believe that machines are efficient, easy to control, and hard to destroy. In his classical treatment of bureaucracy, Max Weber (1978, pp. 987–989) observed:

> Once fully established, bureaucracy is among those social structures which are hardest to de-stroy. . . . The ruled, for their part, cannot dispense with or replace the bureaucratic apparatus once it

exists, for it rests upon expert training, a functional specialization of work, and an attitude set on habitual virtuosity in the mastery of single yet methodically integrated functions. . . .

Such an apparatus makes "revolution" in the sense of forceful creation of entirely new formations of authority, more and more impossible—technically, because of its control over the modern means of communication . . . and also because of its increasingly rationalized inner structure.

A bureaucracy places more value on its own survival and stability than on performing its function satisfactorily. Government bureaucracies are able to survive despite their inefficient delivery of services because they are subsidized and the size of their subsidies does not depend on their performance. Rather, their survival depends on their size and ability to serve the political purposes of the people or agencies who provide their subsidies. According to W. A. Niskanen (1971, pp. 8, 11) budget maximization is the driving force behind government bureaucracies. For them, growth is survival insurance:

In fifty years, [U.S.] government expenditures have grown eighty-fold, from an eighth to a third of the gross national product (GNP). Even when adjusting by subtracting expenditures for national defense and veterans' benefits, the growth pattern remains unchanged. Per capita expenditures, adjusted in this manner and expressed in constant dollars, have increased more than five-fold during the period. . . . Since 1949 the government work force has grown at a compounded annual rate of 3.4 percent, more than twice that of the population as a whole (1.4 percent) and almost twice that of private sector employment (1.8 percent).

The operations of an ideal bureaucracy, like those of an ideal machine, never vary and are independent of the environment. As Weber (1978, p. 988) observed: "The professional bureaucrat is chained to his activity in his entire economic and ideological existence. In the great majority of cases he is only a small cog in the ceaselessly moving mechanism which prescribes to him an essentially fixed routine of march." Therefore, as long as a bureaucracy's subsidy does not vary, neither will the quality or quantity of its output. Increased productivity is not one of its objectives. For this reason, managers of bureaucracies focus on inputs rather than outputs; inputs are easier to measure and control. They assume that the control of costs is equivalent to the control of performance.

Because bureaucracies induce machinelike behavior in their members, they suppress people's need to express themselves as purposeful individuals:

> Though man is rational, he is also biological and emotional. He proceeds not only by his wits but by his instinct, his intuition, and his feelings. And though he is political and social, he is also a single person and idiosyncratic. He has peculiar personal needs and fears and desires, and retains a sense of himself alone. Though he has an urge for order and safety, he also persists in inconsistency and the disorderly and even dangerous conduct out of which come many of the truly imaginative and original works of man. Within the bureaucratic system is a spirit antagonistic to this part of man. It is this, I think, that produces the bitter and sardonic tones that so often appear when people speak of bureaucratic action [Morison, 1966, p. 64].

As a result, employees of bureaucracies become inflexible and indifferent to those they serve.

Bureaucracies affect the performance of an organization as a whole as well as the individuals within:

> Something happens to a plan of action or a program when you enclose it in an institute, or in this case, in a bureau. It tends to lose its freshness, its responsiveness, within the hard and rigid lines of the institution. Those at work on the program tend to get caught in complicated struggles for power and place within the structure and may for-

get the purpose for which they exist. . . . Any institution, any department, any bureau that gets lost
in its own concerns loses its awareness and responsiveness to the outside situations it is supposed to
deal with [Morison, 1966, p. 64].

Bureaucracies resist adaptation and, therefore, can operate efficiently only in static environments. Today, however, because their environments are increasingly changing, they are less
and less able to perform acceptably. When their survival is
threatened, they usually demand even stricter-than-usual adher-
ence to their rules and regulations, both internally and externally. This further reduces their efficiency, effectiveness, and
concern for the people they are supposed to serve.

Conclusion

Sooner or later a monopoly's or a bureaucracy's cost of
providing a service exceeds the service's value to those who pay
for it. Because consumers of publicly provided services usually
do not pay for them directly or have no alternative sources, the
excessive cost is not apparent. However, the poor quality of
service usually is. Monopolies and bureaucracies are seldom
grateful for the demand that justifies their existence; they tend
to treat their consumers with disdain and disrespect, habitually
delaying and otherwise inconveniencing those who come for the
service that is their due.

As long as consumers of services do not feel that they
are receiving value for their money or feel mistreated by those
who provide the services, they will not convert their desire for
services into a demand for them. Without a greater-than-expected
increase in demand, employment in services cannot increase
enough to significantly reduce unemployment. Therefore, the
problem of how to provide services efficiently and effectively
can be reformulated into three parts:

1. How can service agencies operated or controlled by govern-
    ment be debureaucratized and demonopolized or be re-

placed by nonbureaucratic, nonmonopolistic private agencies?

2. What can corporations do, with or without the required changes in government service agencies, to increase employment in businesses providing goods or services?

3. What can the public do to increase the likelihood of instituting the changes required in the provision of services?

It is to these questions that Part Two is devoted.

5

Making Government Responsive and Efficient

In this chapter we shall consider what governments can do to convert the service sector, which is generally perceived as wealth consuming, to a wealth-producing part of the economy and thereby provide the jobs required to solve the unemployment problem. A wealth-producing service sector would have to be consumer oriented and capable of continually increasing its productivity—that is, it would have to be effective and increasingly efficient. We propose two strategies to bring about the necessary conversion: (1) debureaucratizing and demonopolizing the service sector and (2) improving the quality of work life in government service agencies. We shall consider each of these strategies in turn.

Debureaucratizing and Demonopolizing the Service Sector

In order to create an increasingly productive, consumer-oriented service industry, it must be debureaucratized and demonopolized. To this end we propose that governments do five things:

1. Turn over to the private sector the provision of as many public services as possible.
2. Where possible, require consumers to pay directly for the services they receive.

3. Where consumers are not able to pay for the services they need, subsidize the consumers, *not* the providers.
4. Create as many competing public and private sources as possible.
5. Where a supplier must be subsidized, base the subsidy on the amount and quality of service rendered.

Government Unloading. In his book *Privatizing the Public Sector,* Savas (1982, pp. 110-111) observed:

> It is evident that with few exceptions, little rigorous research has been done to evaluate and compare public and private provision of services. Nevertheless, the few robust studies . . . indicate that private provision is superior to public provision of these services.
>
> It is safe to say, at least, the public provision of services is not superior to private provision, while those who believe that private services are best can find considerable support for their position.

Therefore, governments should turn over to the private sector as many services as they can.

Private service agencies should be allowed and encouraged to bid against public agencies for the right to provide services where only one agency can serve at a time. For example, private companies should be allowed to bid for contracts to collect trash, maintain roads, provide emergency ambulance service, and operate libraries and even schools.

Recall from Chapter Four that privately collected trash in Newark, New Jersey, saves that city a considerable amount of money each year. Several years ago there was a prolonged strike of trash collectors in a suburban Newark township. The township's government solicited bids from private firms. Of the several bids submitted, every one offered the service at a significant savings.

Bids submitted by public and private agencies should be opened publicly. Contracts should be awarded for relatively short periods, no more than five years, to prevent bureaucratization of the serving agency.

It should be noted that the U.S. Postal Service, whose services have been deteriorating for years, now has strong competition from private delivery services:

> In this activity [delivering small packages] the parcel post service of the U.S. Postal Service has a very strong competitor, namely the United Parcel Service (UPS), a private, profit-making, worker-owned enterprise.
>
> Evidence as to their relative performance is indirect, but the following reports are suggestive: (1) UPS handles twice as many parcels as the Postal Service; (2) UPS is faster—a parcel mailed by parcel post from Washington to Los Angeles takes more than eight days, or longer than a Pony Express trip from Missouri to California in 1861; (3) UPS rates are generally cheaper; (4) the damage rate at UPS is one-fifth that of the Postal Service; (5) UPS insures every parcel up to $100 without an extra charge; (6) UPS keeps a record of each parcel; (7) UPS will pick up parcels from the mailer, for a fee; (8) UPS makes three delivery attempts, compared with one by the Postal Service; (9) in 1972 UPS earned an after-tax profit of $77 million, whereas the Postal Service lost $300 million on its tax-free parcel post business. . . .
>
> The ultimate indignity was suffered by the Postal Service when the General Services Administration urged all federal agencies to reduce their mail costs by using commercial carriers [Savas, 1982, p. 98].

In addition, private companies like Federal Express and Purolator have virtually taken over the express-mail business. Furthermore, as we indicated in Chapter Four, electronic mail, also privately carried, is rapidly replacing normal mail because of its greater reliability.

In Philadelphia, the current cost of providing a child with what is widely acknowledged as a poor public education exceeds the cost of sending a child to the best private school in the area. This fact obviously supports the privatization of schools.

In Mexico, the nationalized airline, Aeromexico, consistently lost money and provided poor service, while the private airline, Mexicana, made a profit and provided much better service. However, the Mexican government recently nationalized Mexicana Airlines. It is now unprofitable and its service has deteriorated noticeably.

Where it is not possible for a government to turn over all of a service to the private sector, it should turn over as much as possible:

> Institutional arrangements should be chosen so that government is involved in only a minimal way or not at all. By this rule one would prefer market arrangements for private goods (e.g., private day-care facilities), market or franchise arrangements for toll goods (e.g., lease or sale of municipal utilities such as water supply, and recreational facilities such as tennis courts), and voluntary service or collective goods (e.g., ambulance service in small communities) [Savas, 1982, p. 124].

When government permits private agencies to provide some of a public service, competition is created. This makes public and private competitors more attentive to their productivity and to consumer satisfaction. The more competitors, the more responsive they are likely to be to consumers.

Direct Payment by Consumers. Where a service is provided by a public or private agency, consumers benefit when they can select a source and pay directly. "Efficiency is more likely to be realized when there is a direct link between paying for the service and realizing its benefits, and the customer has an economic incentive to shop wisely" (Savas, 1982, p. 83).

Many publicly provided services for which there are no direct charges are misused or abused by their users; an example is the cleanup of solid waste in the United States. The cost of disposing of products and their packaging is completely concealed from producers and consumers and thus is ignored by them. If each product marketed were taxed at the point of production by an amount that would cover the cost of its eventual disposal, producers would try to minimize this cost, such as by using larger containers, recyclable materials, and less superfluous packaging. Consumers, who eventually have to pay this disposal cost, would be motivated to purchase items that minimize this cost, especially if this cost was clearly indicated on each product or package.

Subsidizing Consumers, Not Suppliers. When service agencies are subsidized to provide a service regardless of the amount and quality of service provided, they have little or no incentive to perform efficiently or effectively. This can be avoided by having the recipients of a service pay directly for it. However, in many cases people who need a service cannot pay for it. In such cases it is better for the government to subsidize the users rather than the providers. An effective way of doing this was developed for public education by Christopher Jencks (1970) of Harvard University, who proposed a *voucher system*.

In R. L. Ackoff's version of this system (Ackoff, 1974, chap. 5), the parents of each school-age child would be given an educational voucher worth a specified amount of money payable by the government to the school. The voucher would cover the tuition for *any* public school and transportation, if required, or part or all of the tuition for a private school under the conditions described below. Students or their parents acting for them could apply to any school for admission without being constrained by location or political jurisdiction.

Public schools that received more applications than they could accommodate would select from the applicants as follows: They would have to accept old students and new applicants who lived in their designated areas; *the rest would be randomly selected.* This would provide students with assured access to the school nearest to them and "equal" access to any other school, that is, equal to that of other out-of-district students. The problem of desegregating schools would thus be eliminated.

Public schools would have no source of income other than that obtained by cashing the vouchers they received. If they failed to attract and retain enough students to cover their costs, *they would go out of business.* Private schools could charge whatever they wanted, but parents would have to pay or be paid by the school the difference (if any) between the charges and the value of the voucher. These schools would be permitted to redeem vouchers only if they selected new applicants at random.

Clearly, the voucher system would create competition between public and private schools as well as between public schools. It would also encourage differences between schools. Specialization as needed would take place. For example, if a large number of retarded or deaf children required specialized education, some schools would provide it, especially if vouchers for the handicapped had a higher value than those for normal students.

Under a voucher system, educators would obtain forceful feedback from students and their parents. As a result, they would learn more from their successes and failures and become more adaptive. Schools would tend to be more responsive to the needs and desires of their communities. Their administrators would be likely to involve parents and students in the management of the schools, probably by creating local school boards.

E. S. Savas (1982, pp. 68-69) cites a number of other services for which vouchers are already used: food stamps, college tuition vouchers issued under the GI Bill of Rights after World War II, Medicaid and Medicare vouchers, and cultural vouchers.

> How should government help poor people get enough to eat?
>
> (a) *Give them food.* That would require a costly, clumsy national distribution system. Even then, mothers desperate for powdered milk would all too often get cornmeal instead.
>
> (b) *Give them money for food.* Some recipients would spend the money on beer or bingo—not many, but enough to create a stink and give the program a black eye.
>
> (c) *Give them vouchers, funny money usable only for food.* The right answer, as shown by 15 years' experience, is (c). Society has settled, with great success, on food stamps. . . .
>
> The idea of helping poor people pay for housing with vouchers is validated by the largest controlled experiment in history.

It ran from 1973 to 1980, covered 30,000
families in twelve cities and cost $160 million. Stu-
dents of the test, like Prof. Bernard Frieden of
M.I.T., regard it as a substantial success. Much better than other kinds of Federal housing assistance,
it reached the very poor ["Funny Money and the
Poor," 1983, p. A30].

Vouchers could also be used by neighborhoods or communities
to purchase services such as street cleaning or street repair from
public or private sources.

Competitive Sources of Services. Voucher and direct-
payment systems will have their desired effects on the quality
and cost of services only if there are several competing service
providers: "The degree of competition that an arrangement permits will, to a significant degree, determine how efficiently that
arrangement will supply a service" (Savas, 1982, pp. 80-81).

As the preceding discussion of vouchers reveals, competition between public agencies can be developed by making the
income of each agency depend on the amount and quality of
service that it provides. When such agencies are also required to
compete with private agencies, as would be the case in a voucher
school system, they are even further motivated to perform efficiently and effectively.

Tolls collected for using bridges, tunnels, and highways
are a familiar type of direct payment for service. Unfortunately,
alternative facilities for such services, where they exist, are
usually operated by a government monopoly, and therefore
there is uniform pricing. This is the case in New York City,
which has been described as an island completely surrounded by
toll booths. For many years, the Tacony-Palmyra Bridge, con-
necting Philadelphia to New Jersey, was privately owned and
operated. It charged one fifth as much as nearby government-
operated bridges.

Where a single entity, whether public or private, controls
several sources of a service, each should be operated as a profit
center with freedom to set its own prices, and the compensation
of its employees should be proportional to its profitability. This
is what was done in the very successful Super Fresh chain of

supermarkets, which is replacing the older centrally controlled and unsuccessful A&P stores (see Chapter Eight).

Subsidizing Services, Not Servers. Subsidized budgets of government service agencies have a tendency to grow independently of the amount and quality of service provided. Clearly, their subsidies should be based on both factors. For example, the universities in Ontario receive a government subsidy proportional to the number of students they serve. Different amounts are provided for different types of student, for example, undergraduate and graduate. This way of determining the size of subsidies is most effective where there are competing sources of providing a service, as there are in Ontario's system of higher education. But even where this is not the case, subsidizing service rather than the server is desirable because it precludes the growth of monopolistic government service agencies.

Summary. The five measures proposed here for demonopolizing and debureaucratizing the provision of services would pressure public and private service agencies to serve their consumers efficiently and effectively. These measures would help produce a service sector that created more value than it consumed. The more it did so, the more demand there would be for its outputs. The more demand for its outputs, the more employment this sector could provide.

Improving Work Life in Service Agencies

The word *service* still retains strong echoes of its origin in the Latin word *servus,* meaning "slave." *Servitium* was the work expected of slaves and hence was not expected to be performed by the free or the freed. The Christian revolution, which aimed to raise the value of the services of the slave to the highest rank, invoked Matthew 20:16: "So the last shall be first, and the first last: for many be called, but few chosen." The Roman pontiff came to call himself "the servant of the servants of God." The notion that service is the highest form of human effort was thus added to that of service as work fit only for slaves.

This paradox has survived endless reformations, revolutions, and rebellions. To serve is still taken to be demeaning unless it is exalting. What transforms slavelike labor into exalted service is the amount of skill required to provide it, the nature of the need or desire served, the relationship between the server and the served, and prevailing religious, moral, and social opinion.

Service runs the entire gamut of useful effort. In the political sphere, it ranks as the highest accomplishment of political office. On the other hand, domestic service still carries much of its original Roman connotation, slave labor.

Other forms of human endeavor contrast with service. The most important are craftsmanship and its elevated counterpart, art. These were and are the work of free people, and they differ from service in another important respect. Arts and crafts result in tangible products; service produces only effects. In materialistic societies, the products of arts and crafts generally have a higher social standing than the effects of services. For these reasons, necessary forms of social service seek to align themselves with arts and crafts, such as law, medicine, and architecture.

These sociopsychological aspects of service are directly relevant to any effort to raise its quality and to increase the productivity of service workers. The status attributed to these workers largely reflects the status they attribute to themselves. Their self-esteem is greatly affected, in turn, by the quality of their work lives. Therefore, the quality of their work lives affects the quality and productivity of their work. Therefore, to improve the quality of service and reduce its costs, service providers must be provided with a satisfying work life.

The movement in MDCs toward increasing work satisfaction is growing and developing rapidly and has been given particular impetus by the Japanese (for example, see Jenkins, 1981; Trist, 1981). However, this movement has focused more on production industries than services and hence more on the private sector than the public. Nevertheless, its concepts are applicable to both.

The quality-of-work-life (QWL) movement has evolved through eight stages: (1) worker control of the work environment, (2) job rotation, (3) work enrichment, (4) the combination of job rotation and work enrichment, (5) career planning and personal-problem solving, (6) semiautonomous work groups, (7) participative democracy, and (8) integration into the community. We shall consider each of these in turn.

Worker Control of the Work Environment. In this process, management turns over to the workers at least some decisions that affect the work environment but not the work done and how they do it. For example, workers may be given control over the kind of food served in the lunch room, the design of their locker rooms, the content of the company newspaper, or the kind of recreational facilities provided. In some cases workers are allowed to determine their working hours, but not total work time. In other cases the amount of work expected of a worker per day is specified, and whenever this is completed, the worker may leave. Workers may also be given a choice of benefits and the ability to change their choices as their needs change.

This relinquishment of managerial matters not directly work related has usually increased work satisfaction and productivity, at least for a while. Eventually, however, the novelty wears off, as most changes desired by the workers are made. Then their job satisfaction and productivity level off and in some cases decline. For this reason, it has become clear that maintaining (let alone improving) job satisfaction and productivity requires more than controlling the work environment; something must be done about work itself.

Job Rotation. In most production labor, a simple task is performed repeatedly. To reduce the boredom that derives from such work, workers are allowed to rotate among different tasks. Their productivity may decrease while they learn new tasks, but job satisfaction increases, and once the tasks are learned, productivity rises. It takes longer to become bored with a set of different tasks, but if each task is boring in itself, boredom eventually sets in and productivity levels off or declines. This leads to the redesign of individual tasks to make them more satisfying.

Work Enrichment. In this process, work itself is redesigned to better fit the workers. In the past, workers adapted to fit tasks that machines could not do or could not do economically. In contrast, in work enrichment designs, tasks are adapted to fit people. Tasks are made as complex as workers can handle. In some cases, individual workers produce or assemble a complete product or subassembly.

"Quality circles," now widely publicized, provide a way of enriching work. They give workers the responsibility of monitoring, correcting, and improving quality; in some cases, workers can stop production when the quality of output is unacceptable. Such responsibilities require training and technical skills, which in turn raise the status of the work. Quality circles also involve workers in decision making, thus enhancing their self-image.

No matter how complex a task is, if it is repeated over and over again, it eventually becomes boring and unsatisfying. It is for this reason that the concepts of job rotation and work enrichment were combined.

The Combination of Job Rotation and Work Enrichment. In this stage of the QWL movement, the worker is rotated among a set of enriched tasks. This postpones the point at which boredom is reached; however, unless the tasks are changed before this point, dissatisfaction eventually returns. To change the complex tasks to which workers are assigned requires that they learn new skills. This, in turn, requires a great deal of training, which calls attention to the personal development of individual workers.

Career Planning and Personal-Problem Solving. Most workers want to develop their capabilities and move up the organizational ladder. Therefore, some organizations encourage employees to prepare personal development plans and review them with career counselors who help the workers to realize their aspirations. Such plans frequently require education outside the organization. This is partially or fully paid for by the employer.

In career planning, employees are treated as individuals, their unique preferences and aspirations are acknowledged, and employers help employees to achieve their aspirations.

What happens to employees in their non-work-related lives often affects their performance at work. Non-work-related problems can reduce productivity, and problems at work can exacerbate personal problems. Because of this, many organizations provide *employee assistance programs,* through which any employee with a work-related or personal problem can get the help of an expert counselor and, if necessary, professional treatment (see *Employee Assistance Program: A Model,* 1981). These programs deal with alcoholism, drug addiction, marital problems, financial difficulties, and so on. Moreover, some of these programs are available to all members of employees' immediate families. The employer's insurance usually covers all or most of the cost associated with providing this assistance.

Evaluative studies of employee assistance programs reveal that they are not only humane but increase employee satisfaction with work and productivity. For example, in 1973 a large aerospace company initiated such a program. Over the next five years, 800 of its 17,000 employees used the service to treat the following range of problems: alcoholic, emotional, family, drug-related, legal, financial, and gambling. An alcohol rehabilitation program run by the U.S. Navy has reduced sick days and personal injuries, as well as the cost to the navy of inpatient care.

Semiautonomous Work Groups. The concept of work has been further enriched by considering a group rather than an individual as the basic working unit. Such groups are given as complex a set of tasks as they can handle and a set of performance objectives. They are then free to organize themselves and their work environment however they see fit. The establishment of such semiautonomous work groups frequently eliminates the lowest level of supervision; groups manage themselves, and a manager coordinates the activities of several groups. In some cases these groups can negotiate with each other for the exchange of tasks or personnel.

Semiautonomous work groups are given almost complete control over the means they employ to accomplish objectives set by a higher authority. Therefore, the next conceptual leap came when workers were given the right to participate in setting these objectives and in formulating the policies that affect them.

Participative Democracy

Democratization of the work place consists of giving workers a role in making decisions and setting the policies that affect them. Initially, such participation was relatively innocuous, but it has become substantial over time. Originally restricted to communication, it has evolved through consultation to actually taking part in decision making.

Communication. Worker participation begins with improved communication. Workers are given more effective ways to transmit their ideas and feelings to management. Suggestion boxes, opinion and attitude surveys, and informal discussions between superiors and subordinates are used for this purpose. In addition, management informs workers about the organization's activities and performance. This is usually done regularly either orally or in writing.

Consultation. As a result of improved communication, managers began to consult workers and solicit their suggestions and advice on issues that could affect the workers. Management usually need not take the workers' advice, but it is taken into account. If the advice is rejected, some explanation of the rejection is expected.

Decision making. In the strongest form of participation, the workers have a voice in making decisions that affect them. This is usually referred to as "codetermination." Arrangements for such participation vary widely and are still being developed. They range all the way from placing worker representatives on corporate boards to collective decision making at the work level. In general, the latter has been found to be more effective than the former (Emery and Thorsrud, 1969). In a completely democratic organization, any one who has control over others is in turn controlled collectively by these others; no one has absolute power.

In an organization where a division of labor is necessary, a hierarchy is needed to coordinate the labor. On the other hand, a democracy is required to maximize the quality of work life and productivity. The trick, therefore, is to synthesize the apparently incompatible concepts of hierarchy and democracy. This can be done in a *circular organization*.

The design of a circular organization has many variations. No two instances of it are exactly the same. It usually has to be adapted to the unique characteristics of the organization involved and its environment.

In a basic circular organization, each manager is provided with a board. Each board except the ones at the top and bottom of the organization consists of (1) the manager of the unit, (2) that manager's immediate superior, and (3) that manager's immediate subordinates. In some cases, managers invite some of their peers and/or outsiders onto their boards, especially when their units are geographically separated from the rest of the organization.

The top board contains the chief executive officer, his or her immediate subordinates, representatives of the external stakeholders, and in some cases representatives from each level of employees, including the bottom. The employee representatives should be elected by their constituencies for a specified term. Terms should be staggered to avoid a complete turnover of board personnel.

The lowest-level boards contain all the nonmanagerial personnel who report to the lowest-level managers, any managers who report to these boards, as well as their immediate superiors. If the lowest-level units are large, the boards could be too large to operate effectively. Therefore, these units should be small, about ten people. Reducing the size of these units need not increase the number of lowest-level managers required. If the lowest-level units are set up as semiautonomous work groups, they can select their own leaders from among themselves. Then no managers are needed at the lowest level, and each work group can have its own board in which all of its members can participate along with the manager to whom the group reports. The board of the lowest-level manager then contains the leaders of the semiautonomous work groups reporting to him and his immediate superior.

Note that through these boards, all managers located at least two levels from the top and bottom interact directly with *five* levels of management: two above (in their superiors' board), two below (in their subordinates' boards), and their own. This interaction makes possible effective coordination of organizational units at the same level and the integration of units at different levels.

What do the boards do? First, each board *coordinates* the activities and plans of the units reporting to the manager whose board it is. Since the managers in these units constitute a majority of each board (with the possible exception of the highest-level board), they essentially coordinate themselves with the assistance of two immediately superior managers.

Second, each board *integrates* the activities and plans of all the units represented on it, assuring their compatibility with higher-level and lower-level plans and activities. This is facilitated by the fact that the highest-ranking member of each board may be a member of as many as two higher-level boards, and the lowest-ranking members may participate in as many as two lower-level boards.

Third, each board has *policy-making* and *planning* responsibility for the unit reporting to it. A policy is a *rule* that governs decision making; it is not a decision in the ordinary sense. For example, a board might establish a policy of promotion from within, but the decision to promote a particular individual remains the responsibility of the manager. Boards make policies; managers make decisions. Boards also supervise and participate in the planning of the units whose managers report to it.

The policies and plans made by any board must be consistent with those of higher-level boards. However, a board can ask for a change of a policy or plans made by a higher-level board through its senior members or, if it is a policy of the top board, through its representatives on that board. Note that each board contains the managers of those units that are most affected by the policies and plans it makes. Therefore, the impacts of these policies and plans on other levels are not likely to escape a board's attention.

The policies made by any board should not deal with contracts between management and organized labor unless the manager whose board it is deals with them. Obviously, many of the problems that come up in such negotiations can be avoided by lower-level board activities. More important, when union members participate in management's policy making and planning, an opportunity is created to convert labor-management negotiations from collective bargaining to collaborative problem solving. We discuss this conversion in Chapter Six.

The question of whether union officials should be permitted to serve as representatives of the workers on the top or intermediate boards cannot be answered in general. It depends on each organization. Such involvement of union officials can facilitate the conversion of collective bargaining to joint problem solving.

The fourth, most controversial, and frequently omitted responsibility of each board is *selection of the manager who reports to it.* Managers may not hold their positions without the approval of their boards and therefore of their immediate subordinates, who constitute a majority of that board. However, a manager's board, except the one at the top, cannot fire that manager—only an immediate superior can do this—but a board can remove the manager from his or her position. Therefore, managers require the approval of both their immediate superiors and their immediate subordinates. This is what makes the circular organization design democratic: Every manager is subject to the collective control of those over whom he or she has direct control. Authority flows up as well as down. This reduces the chances that it will be exercised arbitrarily.

A manager's staff requires special attention. Staff members can participate in management in the following way. All managers who have staffs either designate chiefs of staff or perform these roles themselves. A board is then formed for each chief of staff. It includes this chief, the manager to whom he or she reports (unless the chief is the manager), and the staff members. The board operates just as other boards do, but its domain is the work of the staff, not management. It fills the position of chief of staff, not the managerial position. It sets policy for staff work and coordinates and integrates with other staff units. The chief of staff may be a member of the manager's board.

Now consider a few of the more important characteristics of the circular organization.

How much of a manager's time is consumed by boards? This obviously depends on the number of boards on which he or she serves. In general, but not without exception, a manager ought to have fewer than ten people reporting directly. Few boards meet for as much as four hours per month; most meet for two hours or less. Then, if a manager is on ten boards (and most are on fewer) at most forty hours per month would be spent at board meetings—no more than 25 percent of the normal work week.

Although this leaves a good deal of time for other activities, this is not the point. The point is that most of a manager's responsibilities can be fulfilled through participation on these boards. They enable the manager to plan and formulate policies, to coordinate and integrate the work done under him, to evaluate subordinates and their subordinates, to inform and motivate these people, and to keep abreast of what is going on above, below, and on his own level. These constitute the largest part of a manager's job.

Each board should develop its own procedural rules. Some, for example, have the highest-ranking member serve as chairman; others rotate this position. Some meet regularly; others on call. Most set up a procedure by which anyone or a subset of board members can initiate a session. A great deal depends on how dispersed the members of a board are.

Few boards use majority rule. They usually operate by consensus. Consensus is an agreement to act in a particular way even though there may be no agreement as to which way is best. Where consensus cannot be obtained, most boards resort to a test of the alternatives under consideration. Then consensus only need be reached on the design of the test. However, the board members must agree to abide by the outcome of the test.

It is important to reemphasize that these boards are *not* management committees. They do not make decisions for the units reporting to them. However, managers usually use their boards in an advisory capacity, although they are under no obligation to do so.

The circular organization design has been used in a number of public and private organizations, some very large, others small. It has often been used in parts of an organization without being used by the whole. Its implementation has usually been gradual and sequential, often initiated one level at a time. We know of no application of the design in which those affected felt that morale and performance did not improve significantly. In no case of which we are aware has the design been implemented and subsequently abandoned.

An example of a modified circular organization is described in Chapter Eight.

Integration into the Community. In work enrichment, the concept of *work* was enlarged. In semiautonomous work groups, the concept of the *worker* was enlarged. Most recently the concept of the *work place* has been enlarged. The employing organization is taken as a part of a larger community that it can affect and be affected by significantly. Awareness of this has led to the formation of *community councils*, usually consisting of representatives of government, employers, employees, and the general public. These councils consider issues that affect the community's ability to provide an environment conducive to satisfying and productive work and nonwork activities. Jamestown, New York, pioneered this development in the United States (Eldred, 1978).

In the early 1970s the manufacturing community of Jamestown was in decline. It had a reputation for strained labor relations and local companies were plagued by strikes. This did nothing to attract new industry. Congressman Stanley Lundine, who was then mayor of Jamestown, discussed the situation with representatives of both labor and management. They quickly organized to deal with the threat to industry, jobs, and community.

In February 1972, the Jamestown Labor Management Committee met for the first time. As a result of its continued efforts, unemployment in the region was cut in half, certain existing industries expanded, and Cummins Engine, another manufacturer, moved in.

One final note on productivity and quality of work life. Improvement in productivity can obviously also be obtained by introducing new technology, but the amount of improvement that can be obtained in this way depends on the attitudes of the workers. If they are hostile to these changes, workers can minimize the effects of modernization. How workers affect the incorporation of new technology depends on the extent to which their interests and opinions are taken into account when designing and implementing its introduction. These interests and opinions are best taken into account if workers participate in the planning of innovations. The payoff of such programs is more than increased productivity and job satisfaction, even more than better plans; it also consists of increased flexibility and responsiveness. Without flexibility and responsiveness, an organization cannot remain vital, let alone vigorous, in a changing environment.

Conclusion

In Chapter Four we argued that there is an increasing desire for services. This desire is not being converted into as much demand as is possible because many services are not worth their current cost and are of too low a quality. If they were less expensive and of higher quality, enough jobs could be created in the service sector to significantly reduce, if not eliminate, the unemployment problem.

Government is the largest single provider of services in most MDCs. However, most of its service agencies are bureaucratic monopolies that provide services at too high a cost and too low a quality. These conditions do not induce conversion of a desire for services into a demand for it. Therefore, government service agencies must be demonopolized and debureaucratized. We suggested two ways this could be done.

First, move as many public services into the private sector as possible, make all public and private service agencies compete for customers, and make the incomes of these agencies depend on the amount and quality of service they provide. Those public and private service agencies that do not generate enough income to support themselves under these conditions should be allowed to go out of business.

Second, install QWL programs in all service agencies. The quantity and quality of service provided by many service workers, particularly in public agencies, are notoriously low. This is a consequence of the poor quality of work life that their employing organizations provide. By giving service workers an opportunity to redesign their working conditions and the work itself, their productivity and the quality of their work can be increased significantly.

A few local, state, and federal governments have made moves in these directions. But the measures we propose are not ones that most governments are anxious to take precisely because governments themselves are bureaucratic monopolies that resist change. In this chapter we consider how government can be demonopolized and debureaucratized. In the next chapter, we consider how individual corporations can create more jobs, regardless of what government does.

6

Designing
New Corporate Strategies

In Chapter Five we suggested how the governments of MDCs can change themselves so as to promote the development of wealth-producing, service-based economies. Such development, we believe, would significantly reduce the unemployment problem. However, the effectiveness of such government actions obviously depends on supportive action by corporations. Fortunately, supportive behavior by corporations is in their own best interest whether or not governments act appropriately. Therefore, corporations are likely to adapt to a service-based economy even if they must do so unilaterally. Such adaptation could stimulate complementary moves by governments.

It should be kept in mind that a service-based economy does not imply a decline in industrial production. Recall that the transformation of economies from being agriculturally based to being industrially based did not reduce agricultural production—agricultural production has increased continuously, but the percentage and number of people engaged in agriculture have decreased. The same development can be expected in production industries: Their output will continue to increase, but employment in them will decrease as they become more efficient through mechanization and automation.

Therefore, we propose that corporations get into services, not out of production. In fact, we propose the development of new products and production processes, and the renewal of old

107

ones. This, we believe, can contribute to the economic development of both MDCs and LDCs. Finally, we consider how to increase corporate productivity without displacing employees.

The measures we propose are intended to enable corporations to compete more effectively, to create new employment, and to generate investment capital.

Diversifying into Services

The entry of a product-oriented company into the service sector ought to be as natural, nondisruptive, and uncontrived as possible. This requires finding points of entry that are part of the company's current activities. We shall consider how such points of entry can be identified and what the requirements are for successfully passing through them.

Points of Entry. Natural points of entry into service businesses can be found by offering services that (1) are used by the company itself, (2) are required by the use of its products, or (3) require the use of its products.

Services a company uses. Every company contains units that provide services to other parts of the company. These services are often of high quality and low cost and hence marketable. For example, Mobil Oil, General Electric, and a number of aerospace companies sell their computer-based services to others at a profit. The British branch of Mars Corporation sells the services of its internal market research unit. U.S. Steel provides plant design and management services to LDCs that want to produce their own steel. Martin Marietta has just obtained a contract from the U.S. Department of Energy to manage a complex of nuclear facilities at Oak Ridge, Tennessee, and Paducah, Kentucky. Several multinational oil companies manage and operate refineries owned by LDCs. Temco and Union Carbide rent their training and conference facilities to others. Several airlines provide training programs for personnel of other airlines. A number of companies with their own fleet of trucks provide trucking services to others. This is a particularly advantageous arrangement when the hauling service is provided on return trips that would otherwise be made by empty trucks.

Because companies also use services that are externally provided, they often become very intelligent, discriminating users. This has enabled some companies to acquire an external provider of such a service or to create an internal unit that provides it and then to offer the service to others. For example, a Mexican brewer, one of the largest advertisers in Mexico, developed considerable skill in creating advertising messages and selecting media. It purchased an advertising agency that served it, expanded and improved its services, and offered these services to others. Later, this company purchased some of the television stations it used and improved them as well.

A manufacturer of heavy equipment purchased a credit company so it could finance the inventories of its distributors and the purchases of its products from them. It then successfully marketed these services to other equipment producers, distributors, and their customers.

Services required by use of the company's products. Many companies profitably service their own products, such as IBM, General Electric, Xerox, and Sears. The efficient services they provide also improve the marketability of their products.

> IBM, which became the biggest seller of personal computers within two years of entry into the market, is now considering using its technology and financial resources to take a major role in the related software business, company and industry sources report.
>
> The world's largest computer company, which currently distributes several brands of software for its popular IBM PC, is exploring the possibility of buying a stake in some of the companies that write those programs, the sources said [Schrage, 1984, p. F1].

A number of utilities service equipment that uses their product, often through annual contracts. Some producers of small consumer items—for example, lighters, watches, pens, and electric shavers—operate repair facilities in major metropolitan areas. Some manufacturers of uniforms, such as those worn by hospital and supermarket personnel, provide laundering and cleaning services, picking up soiled uniforms from users and delivering clean ones.

Some manufacturers of equipment rent the equipment to users and supply the materials needed for its use. For example, Cory provides equipment for making coffee in offices and regularly provides the coffee and other supplies needed.

Services requiring use of the company's products. Many products are used in providing services; for example, taxi companies and car rental services use automobiles. If a producer of automobiles becomes involved in providing taxi services, it is abler to design its product to fit this use better. Volvo has done just this. Food producers who also operate restaurants, like Stouffer's, are in an advantageous position to produce food for use by restaurants and institutions.

Requirements for Successful Services. A successful service, like a successful product, requires uniqueness and must provide good value. Innovation and effectiveness in the service sector has three principal sources: (1) correction of a deficiency in an existing service, (2) satisfaction of a need or desire not satisfied by any existing service, and (3) exploitation of service opportunities created by a new product.

Correction of a service deficiency. Among the common deficiencies found in services are inconvenience in their use, excessive time to gain access to them or have them provided, unreliability, limited choice, and excessive cost.

Consolidated home repair and maintenance services have been replacing separate plumbing, carpentry, painting, and electrician companies because the consolidated companies provide and coordinate these related trades. This increases convenience. Likewise, special buses to shopping centers and places of entertainment provide convenience, as do credit cards. Two-way radios replaced call boxes in taxis because they reduced waiting time. Federal Express has taken a good deal of the Post Office's business because it delivers mail and small packages more quickly and reliably. Bonded housecleaning teams that come with their own equipment and supplies get the job done quickly and efficiently. Guaranteed services are generally more reliable; they certainly create an expectation of greater reliability. Cable TV provides its users with a wider choice of programs than network TV and often gives a clearer picture. Cinemas that have been divided into several smaller theaters offer a wider choice of movies.

Shops specializing in automobile painting, muffler replacement, and transmission repair often reduce the cost of these services significantly. Health maintenance organizations (HMOs) increase convenience by providing one-stop shopping for health services, often at a relatively low cost.

One of the most successful and creative ways of entering the service sector is by assembling and organizing related but previously independent services into a *service system*. Donald A. Schon (1971, pp. 74-75) provided a number of examples of such systems. Here are a few of them:

> Firms have grown up around "institutional feeding." They take on the function of providing meals to specification for certain numbers of people in certain institutions (hospitals, schools, airliners, hotels). They control not only the purchasing of raw materials, the preparation of intermediates, and the final preparation, but the design and manufacturing of equipment, utensils, and maintenance equipment. They may be integrated back to agriculture, if that seems desirable, or to the steel in their forks. They retain at each point the freedom to decide to make or buy, own or franchise, employ one supplier or a number. Such a firm stands an excellent chance of orchestrating the various innovations required to transform the feeding system. If the economic use of infrared ovens depends, for example, on the uniform slicing of meat to certain thicknesses, the firm can assure that uniformity. . . .
>
> A Danish pastor builds a business around a "recreation system." A travel service provides customers for a chain of hotels and restaurants dotted through Europe; bus and airline companies convey travelers from Denmark to these resorts and back; and a central computer-based information system makes reservations, projects demands, schedules

trips, calculates costs. Control over *each* of these elements allows one to serve as customers for the other, permits full utilization of facilities, reduces costs—and leads, in turn, to increased demand. . . .

RCA in Italy operates an "entertainment system" whose elements include: a "managing firm" which holds contracts for musicians and artists and manages their careers; recording studios, record and tape companies; chains of retail shops for records and tapes; a television station; a firm specializing in installing stereophonic tape recorders in automobiles.

Another example is the recent integration of a wide variety of financial services by Merrill Lynch, Prudential, and Sears.

Satisfaction of an unfilled need or desire. Many people would like to entertain at home without going to the trouble of preparing a good meal and cleaning up afterwards. Takeout foods are not of high enough quality for this purpose and are often an inconvenience. Recognizing this, a company in California was formed to deliver hot catered meals to homes, ready to serve. Table settings are also provided. Later in the evening, everything is removed quickly and unobtrusively.

Some hotels in Europe have recently met previously unfilled needs of traveling executives by providing fully equipped offices with all necessary support services and facilities. Also, air taxi and executive jet services were initiated to meet a need not filled by commercial airlines. Group charter services were similarly conceived.

Creating a new service around a new product. The new personal computer has given rise to a number of new services, including electronic mail networks and software companies. Video cassette players led to cassette rental services, particularly for movies. The videophone, not yet affordable for most companies, is made available by AT&T in videophone conference centers in major cities. New banking services were made available by automated tellers.

The development of new cleaning products and equipment made possible rug, carpet, and furniture cleaning in the home. Some photographers took advantage of the introduction of video cameras to provide videotaping of weddings, anniversaries, and other special events.

Product and Process Development and Redevelopment

No matter how rapidly the service sector grows, the demand for capital and consumer goods will continue to grow. Moreover, the development of the service sector provides opportunities for the development of new products and the redevelopment of old ones.

Equipment and Facilities. As LDCs industrialize, they need production equipment suitable for use by low-skilled labor in labor-intensive processes. The equipment they require should also be easy to maintain. Such equipment is not generally available. LDCs have had no choice but to buy old or new equipment designed for use in MDCs. This equipment incorporates into its design inappropriate assumptions about the relative costs of labor, energy, and capital and the level of skills available for its operation and maintenance.

For example, trucks designed in MDCs incorporate an assumed value of the driver's life. This assumption dictates how much safety equipment the trucks have, which affects their cost. The driver's life cannot be assumed to be infinitely valuable, because there is a limit to how much can be spent for safety. The maximum average amount that can be spent to protect a person's life in a society is based on the person's expected lifetime contribution to national wealth. If more than this were spent for each person, society would go bankrupt. If exactly this amount were spent, nothing would be left for investment. Clearly, this limiting amount varies greatly from society to society. Therefore, a truck designed with safety features that are justified in MDCs is considerably overdesigned for LDC societies. Such overdesign is characteristic of most MDC-produced equipment whose operation poses a danger to its operators or others.

Trucks designed for use in LDCs should also take into account climatic, regulatory, and cultural conditions, which are usually very different from those of MDCs.

To be sure, markets in LDCs may not be large enough

now to justify producing specially designed equipment. Nevertheless, trucks designed for MDCs can be modified and stripped of luxuries to increase their suitability for LDCs. The same is true of most materials-handling, farm, manufacturing, and transportation equipment.

Rural factories in LDCs. Factories in a number of MDCs have been migrating from urban to rural areas for many reasons. There are also good reasons for locating factories in rural areas of LDCs; for example, it helps keep land under cultivation by preventing mass migration from the country to the cities.

A factory built in a rural area of an LDC can be designed to provide services that significantly accelerate rural development. For example, most factories have pumping systems and power-generating facilities that can be used at least during off-hours to distribute water and electricity to farms. Forklift trucks and other materials-handling equipment can be designed to be useful on farms when not in use in the factory; for example, they could be used as small tractors.

Mobile factories in LDCs and MDCs. It is worth reexamining an assumption usually made in designing production facilities: that they should be fixed in one location. A notable exception is in the construction industry, where production equipment is moved from site to site.

It may not be immediately apparent, but these are not the only conditions under which mobile production facilities are justified. For example, efforts to manufacture houses in factories (where their cost is greatly reduced) have often failed because of the constraints imposed on their design by the need to move them from factory to housing site. This is equally true of mobile homes. To overcome these difficulties, General Electric (U.S.A.) built a house-producing facility into a set of truck trailers that could be assembled into a factory on site. Houses could then be manufactured at their site, and their designs were not constrained by transportation requirements. Similarly, a chemical company built a factory on a large barge because its highly mobile customers were almost always located near bodies of water. (Recall the hospital ship *Hope*.)

Food-processing plants that could be moved to where

crops are being harvested would be particularly appropriate for LDCs. Wherever raw material sources or markets vary over time, mobile production facilities may be an advantage.

Distribution systems. In many LDCs, the distribution of products is difficult because much of the population lives in small, remote villages and towns. These communities cannot support retail stores and service centers. Consequently, mobile distribution, sales, and service centers might well be used in LDCs to serve a number of small communities in a region.

In Mexico, CONASUPO, the National Basic Commodity Agency, has mobile food markets that call on small rural communities weekly. Mobile libraries have long been used in this way, even in MDCs. Medical clinics have also been put into vans and trailers. Classrooms for special subjects (such as laboratories and computing facilities) have also been made mobile. Entertainment troupes have long used vehicles to move from community to community, and recently Mercedes announced a mobile executive office.

Automation in MDCs. As previously observed, industrial corporations in MDCs will have to increase their productivity continuously if they are to survive, let alone thrive, in an increasingly competitive free international market. Automation is one of the principal ways in which this can be accomplished. Therefore, the market for automated production and materials-handling equipment will be growing. Mental tasks involving the generation, transmission, processing, storage, and retrieval of information, such as clerical tasks, will also be increasingly automated. Production of equipment for such purposes is already growing rapidly, but it still has a long way to go.

Products. Those LDCs that industrialize successfully will raise their standards of living and therefore consume more goods and services. However, because their standards of living are likely to remain well below those of MDCs for some time, and because their cultures and climates often differ significantly from those of MDCs, many products and services that MDCs try to export to LDCs are inappropriate. Awareness of this is reflected in the widely discussed need for "appropriate technology."

Consider the inappropriateness and excessive cost of Western dress in many LDCs, particularly those in tropical and semitropical climates. The same can be said of many household appliances and furnishings. (There is an old joke about Eskimos using refrigerators to keep their food from freezing.) The design of home appliances and equipment is normally based on an availability and cost of energy that do not apply in LDCs. One result is that foods requiring refrigeration are inappropriate in many LDCs.

Most automobiles are not well suited to LCDs. Their cost is excessive, and they incorporate features that have little or no value to residents of LDCs. Even the smaller four-passenger automobiles are too large for most LDC requirements. Studies carried out in Mexico City in 1976 and in Philadelphia in 1963 both revealed that the average number of passengers in an automobile, including taxis, was 1.2. Less than 15 percent of the vehicles carried more than two people. This suggests that a two-passenger vehicle would serve most needs for private transportation within cities. There is no need for such a vehicle to be able to travel at more than 50 miles per hour.

An appropriately designed two-passenger urban automobile could be sold at no more than about half the price of the least expensive automobile now available. This would considerably enlarge the market for automobiles, even in MDCs. Many communities would welcome such vehicles, because they would reduce congestion and the cost of building and maintaining streets and highways. A study by Sagasti and Ackoff (1971) has shown that if short, narrow, two-passenger vehicles with one passenger seated behind the other were used exclusively in cities, 2.2 times as many people could be accommodated on expressways and from 2.7 to 5.4 times as many on city streets, depending on parking arrangements.

Parking-space requirements would be greatly reduced. For example, a normal U.S. car requires more than 20 feet along a sidewalk for parking. Three of the cars described here would fit into the space required by two conventional automobiles, and additional road space would be available for moving traffic. Parking-space requirements could be further reduced if the doors of the urban automobile either slid along the sides or were placed at front and back. The latter arrangement would permit very dense face-in parking.

Such "urmobiles" would also reduce fuel consumption and pollution due to automobiles. They could be designed to hook on to each other to form trains, to facilitate towing, or to pull others in a nonmotorized cab. Furthermore, their reduced speed and acceleration would make them safer than current vehicles.

Within the last decade there have been a number of prototypes of small urban automobiles. A two-passenger car with a motorcycle engine and fiberglass body is being produced and marketed in France by the Bangor Punta Corporation. In addition, Ford has shown its "concept car," the Cockpit, which is a three-wheel, two-passenger (in tandem) car with one-cylinder engine. It gets over 75 miles per gallon, measures 119 by 66 by 48 inches, and weighs 770 pounds. General Motors' experimental prototype, the TPC ("two-passenger commuter") gets 95 miles per gallon and weighs 1,040 pounds. Early discussions of such vehicles can be found in *Minicar Transit System* (1968) and *Cars for Cities* (1967). Finally, it should be noted that the small trucklike vehicle used by the U.S. Postal Service is the type of vehicle discussed here.

Products for services. Most services require the use of products. Therefore, as services expand, they will require more products. In particular, demand should increase for products associated with such service fields as health, education, communications, and recreation. For those services provided by public agencies, pressure should increase to reduce the cost of the equipment used. This will provide opportunities for product rationalization and development. Innovative products for leisure and recreational use will continue to find a receptive market; such items include the large-headed tennis racket, chess-playing machines, personal computers, and so on.

Although education is a huge business and a major consumer of externally provided facilities, equipment, supplies, and services, there is no single source of supply. More important is the fact that these elements are designed independently of each other. Therefore, the systems resulting from their combination do not consist of well-matched, integrated equipment. For example, a single classroom may use a motion picture projector, a slide projector, an overhead projector, blackboards, pads on easels, a videotape machine and television, and bulletin boards, all for visual displays. An integrated, multipurpose audiovisual system is not available. Thus, there is a great need for a systems approach in the design of educational facilities. Classrooms are usually designed to fit the physical relationship between students and instructor and do not permit rearrangements to suit different types of activities. Perhaps most serious is the fact that schools are designed as single-purpose facilities. As a result, they go unused most of the time. They should be designed to accommodate a large variety of community activities, for adults as well as children. For example, schools could incorporate facilities and services for senior citizens, who could also assist in the educational process. This would be to their and the students' benefit. This would also reduce misbehavior in and abuse of school buildings. Schools could also easily be designed to provide adult educational and recreational programs, especially ones that involved entire families.

Therefore, we believe there are opportunities for corporations to enter the business of developing, producing, and marketing integrated educational systems to schools and school systems.

Productivity

Continuously effective competition in a free market requires continuous increases in productivity. Only those goods-producing corporations that can increase their productivity enough to stave off competition will survive. Furthermore, as competition for services increases, productivity will also become more important in this sector.

Here we consider two of the more important ways of increasing productivity: improving the quality of work life and rationalizing corporate behavior.

Quality of Work Life. The discussion in Chapter Five of ways to improve the quality of work life in government service agencies is equally applicable to production industries. Here we shall focus on an aspect of labor-management relations not discussed there: contract negotiations. This discussion also applies to those government agencies in which the work force is unionized.

Contract negotiations. An adversarial relationship between labor and management is a major obstruction to organizational effectiveness, productivity, and improvement. Conflict between labor and management derives from an assumption made by both: that they are in a win-lose relationship in which either party's gain is the other's loss. Such conflict is intensified when demand for the organization's output declines and jobs become threatened. Many managers believe that such conditions provide them with an opportunity to extract concessions from labor. Indeed, many managers have succeeded in getting them.

Lower wage rates, most managers believe, yield lower costs of labor per unit of output. They tend to overlook the fact that this is only true if the amount of product per unit of labor does not offset the decreased cost of labor per unit of time. It often does. Moreover, even if there is a gain from management's point of view, it is usually short-lived, because labor almost always tries to retract its concessions and make up for them as soon as economic conditions improve. It usually succeeds. (This was the recent experience at Chrysler.) All this intensifies the conflict between labor and management.

Company-union or organization-union contract negotiations are normally carried out by collective bargaining in which interactions are adversarial. Each party formulates its problems before negotiation, identifies its preferred solutions (which almost always entail a loss for the other party), and brings these to the bargaining table in the form of demands. Conflict inevitably follows. The problems to which the demands are addressed are seldom identified or discussed.

In win-win negotiations, problems, not solutions, are brought to the table. Working together, both parties formulate a more general problem that incorporates the perceptions and objectives of each side. They can then try to solve the more general problem jointly to the benefit of each. An example may help clarify this process.

The average daily output of salaried women who carried

out a simple repetitive task had decreased by 20 percent over several years. This threatened the security of the organization. The manager faced the problem alone and came up with a solution: putting the women on piecework and setting the rate so they would have to increase their output by 10 percent to earn the same amount they were making at the time. However, if they increased their output by more than 10 percent, which they were capable of doing, they would earn more.

The manager then converted his solution into a demand, which he made at a collective bargaining session. The women rejected it. The manager threatened to impose piecework whether they approved or not. The women responded by threatening to strike if he did. The bargaining session came to an abrupt end.

The manager called on a consultant for help. The consultant interviewed a number of the women and learned that they had little interest in earning more, but a great deal of interest in working less. Most of the women were married and had children in school, and they wanted more time at home. Consequently, the consultant brought both parties back together and led a joint effort to solve their joint problem. They reached agreement on a definition of a fair day's work as 20 percent more than their current output. They also agreed that the women could leave as soon as they had completed the specified amount of work.

The agreement was implemented. The output rate of the women increased significantly, allowing them to work a much shorter day, as they wanted, and this provided the manager with the higher productivity and lower cost he wanted. Both parties won.

Even when a solution that satisfies both sides is not found, the effort leads to a greater understanding on both sides. Then, whatever conclusion is eventually reached, it is not as likely to be resented by either side as much as a solution proposed by one of the two parties. With joint problem solving, the very concept of sides dissolves over time. Cooperation takes its place.

The management boards described in Chapter Five provide experience in collaborative problem solving and therefore help eliminate adversarial negotiations.

Rationalization of Corporate Processes. Recent comparative studies of Japanese and American productivity indicate that the Japanese advantage lies not so much in lower costs of labor as of management. These studies also indicate that the Japanese have advantages both within and without the organization. We shall now examine ways in which American management can be organized to increase productivity.

Management. The economist Edwin Mansfield (1968) has shown that it takes a surprisingly long time before a new technology is extensively used by industry. Because of this, the quip "Corporations are not doing as well as they know how" rings true. Most corporations are quite casual about exploring and exploiting new technologies, particularly "soft technologies," that is, ways of managing and organizing their activities. Yet, with intensifying international competition, the effectiveness of management and the ability of organizations to learn and adapt are rapidly becoming major determinants of a company's success.

To be sure, much of what is offered to management as a panacea is nothing but fads. Nevertheless, as with hard technology, there is enough of value among the new soft offerings to justify their consideration. Soft technologies provide many opportunities for improvement that are lost or adopted too late.

The uncritical adoption of a new technology is an equally serious mistake. Consider the case of management information systems (MISs). It has been about two decades since these systems came into vogue. Repeated evaluations have shown that most of these systems fail to deliver what managers expect of them. Curiously, the reasons for their disappointing performance are well-known but have had little effect on their design.

The design of these systems has been dictated more by the interests of the technicians who operate them than by the managers who are supposed to be served by them. Put another way, they are designed to maximize the use of computers rather than usefulness to management. For example, a number of studies have shown that managers have a greater need for reducing the amount of *irrelevant* information they receive than for increasing the amount of relevant information. Most managers suffer from a considerable overload of information, a large part of which is irrelevant or useless. Therefore, what they need most in an MIS is *filtration* of irrelevant information and *condensation* of what is relevant and useful. Although computer programs for filtering and condensing information have been available for some time, very few MISs incorporate them.

Managers should play a major role in designing systems that are supposed to serve them. If they feel technically ill equipped to do so, they should learn as much of the relevant technology as is necessary. This is seldom as difficult or time consuming as they imagine. In addition, however these systems are designed, they should be introduced *experimentally* on as small a scale as possible. They should then be evaluated in use by their users before expensive commitments are made. Moreover, they should be designed to make adaptation to changing needs easy.

In contrast to MISs, *management control systems* have been found to be very useful and often exceed the expectations of those they serve. Nevertheless, such systems are relatively rare even though they are easier and less costly to install and use than MISs. In these systems, records are made of the important decisions made by management. These include: (1) how a decision was made and by whom, (2) the information used in making it, (3) the expected effects of the decisions made and when they are expected, (4) the assumptions on which these expectations are based, and (5) who is expected to do what, where, and when to implement the decision.

A management control system then monitors the implementation of the decision, the assumptions on which it is based, and the effects of its implementation. Whenever a significant deviation from what is assumed or expected is observed, the reasons for it are sought and, when found, are used to make corrections. The correction decisions are controlled in the same way as the original decisions. This makes it possible for management *to learn* how to learn and adapt as well as simply to learn and adapt.

Both management control systems and MISs are subsystems of management systems. Management also requires subsystems to assist in problem formulation and decision making.

(For a complete description of a comprehensive management system see Ackoff, 1981, chap. 6.)

Many other examples of failed opportunities for increasing management efficiency and effectiveness could be cited. These occur because few corporations have anyone responsible for keeping up-to-date on developments related to management, for evaluating them, and applying those found to be useful. Just as production engineers have continuing responsibility for upgrading production processes, management scientists should have responsibility for upgrading managerial processes. Nothing can be as costly to a corporation as the obsolescence of these processes.

Intraorganizational relations. Bureaucratic service monopolies are as prevalent in corporations as they are in government. Most corporations contain a number of inefficient and ineffective service units, which obstruct any efforts to measure their performance in order to determine their budgets; these units prefer to be accepted on faith and generously subsidized. Like government bureaucracies, these service units value their survival more than the good performance of their assigned function and believe that their monopolistic growth is insurance against extinction. Therefore, they often exaggerate their personnel requirements and make work to keep their surplus people busy. Unfortunately, the work they make is often unproductive.

Every corporation is handicapped to some extent by administrative red tape and staff units that act as though the function of production units is to support them. They often show an arrogant disregard for the need to satisfy those parts of the corporation that require their services.

Debureaucratization and demonopolization of corporate service agencies are as necessary for decreasing the costs of these agencies and increasing the quality of their output as debureaucratization and demonopolization are in government. As in the case of government, this can be accomplished by requiring these units to operate in a free competitive market. Therefore, they should be profit centers selling their services to both other corporate units that must pay for them directly, but which are permitted to buy them externally, and external customers. An example can help illustrate this.

The chief executive of a major American oil company was concerned with the rapid growth of his corporation's centralized computing facility. (It was one of the largest in the United States at that time.) Units using it did not have to pay. Nevertheless, they complained continuously about poor service. The CEO hired a research organization to measure the value of the center's output so he could determine how much his corporation could justifiably spend on it.

Several months of research directed at objectively placing a value on the center's output was fruitless. Nevertheless, the research revealed that most of the users were dissatisfied with the service and were unable to change it. Their complaints did nothing but evoke excuses from the center. On the other hand, the computing center complained continuously about the unreasonable use and abuse of its services.

These observations led to two recommendations: first, that users of the service be charged for it but be free to purchase such service from external sources if they so desired; second, that the center be required to meet all internal (paid for) requests for its services but be free to sell its services to external users. These recommendations were implemented with dramatic results. The center unloaded one third of its computers. It continued to do virtually all of the internally generated computation, which was now significantly reduced. It also sold a significant portion of its time to external users. Internal users were pleased with the improvement in service, and the center became one of the more profitable units in the company.

The idea contained in this solution has since been applied to a variety of internally provided services with equal success. This experience led to the design of a "multidimensional organization," in which every unit, line, or service is a profit center that operates in an internal as well as an external market economy. A description of this type of organization is given by Ackoff (1981, chap. 7).

Intercorporate Cooperation. Privately owned corporations are, of course, expected to compete in a free economy.

Economic competition is conflict so regulated as to serve the public's interests. Therefore, corporations that are in conflict with each other's objectives are nevertheless in cooperation relative to the public's objectives. Cooperation among them that does not serve the public is considered immoral or illegal. The government is responsible for assuring that the public's interests are well served. Unfortunately, fear of government intervention and retribution discourages corporate efforts at cooperation even where it would serve the public's interests.

To some extent, competitive corporations do cooperate in industrial associations, but almost exclusively in dealing with common noncorporate enemies, including the government, special-interest groups such as consumerists and ecologists, and foreign competition. These associations seldom if ever look for ways in which their members can cooperate legally and morally in both their own and the public's interests. There are a number of ways in which they could do so.

Competitive and noncompetitive companies can cooperate in purchasing goods and services. They can form buying cooperatives or create jointly owned suppliers of research and development, advertising, and trucking, for example. Jointly owned service agencies can serve several companies with economies of scale. The United Parcel Service, the Railway Express Agency, and the Microelectronics and Computer Cooperative in the United States are examples of such intercompany cooperation. The consumer benefits from these because they provide services at lower prices than would otherwise be charged.

For instance, one company may have more production capacity at location A than it needs and less at location B. The converse may be true for another company that uses much the same production technology as the first. The two companies could exchange unused capacity. Some oil companies have been doing something like this for years.

Department stores and producers of goods collaborate when the stores provide concessions to the producers in which they can sell their products. In the automotive industry, shared sales agencies for nondirectly competing makes of cars are already common.

An equipment company that we shall refer to as Able recently found its marketing-distribution system eroding. Unlike its largest competitor, Able did not have a sufficiently complete product line to capture and maintain many exclusive independent distributors. A foreign competitor recently introduced a product line almost as complete as that of the major competitor. This foreign company was infiltrating Able's marketing-distribution system, as well as those of other smaller companies making related products. Because of its low prices and the acceptable quality of its products, the foreign competitor threatened to take over a large part of the marketing-distribution systems of Able and the other smaller companies.

Able designed a marketing-distribution system to serve noncompeting producers of complementary equipment. Their combined product lines were competitive with those of the two giant companies. Moreover, such collaboration opened the possibility of interchanging subassemblies and parts and sharing production facilities and research and development. Able identified its ideal set of collaborators for such a venture and approached them. Much to its surprise and satisfaction, they were receptive. Three companies, each based in a different country, are now jointly engaged in designing a joint venture and in exploring other forms of collaboration.

Although one can cite a number of current examples of intercorporate cooperation, few if any corporations have someone whose primary responsibility is to identify and pursue such opportunities. Business schools certainly do not prepare their students to do this. Professionals with this ability would be particularly useful in Europe, where there are more cultural, political, and economic obstructions to operating across borders than there are within the United States. European multinationals are often victims of economic nationalism and the current worldwide wave of protectionism. They are forced to locate some of their activities within other nations. Cooperation of companies of different national origin often provides a better way of dealing with protectionism.

Corporations working together can influence international, national, and regional development planning and policies. Such a case was recently reported in *The Economist* ("Gyllenhammar's Vigilantes," 1984, p. 67):

> On Saint Valentine's Day, 16 European business leaders will go to Geneva to discuss the massacre of their industries. The European Common Market's commissioner, Viscount Etienne Davignon, will be there, too. The group of (originally 17) industrial big shots, known as G17, was formed a year ago to find ways of meeting growing competition in Europe from American and particularly Japanese companies. . . .
>
> The members of G17 work for companies with combined annual sales of $142 billion. . . . They include the bosses of Philips, Nestlé, Siemens, St. Gobain, and Fiat. The group is chaired by Mr. Pehr Gyllenhammar, chairman of Sweden's Volvo carmaker.
>
> With the help of Paris-based consultants, the group has picked infrastructure, venture capital and/or equity financing and know-how as areas where industry can promote European co-operation. . . .
>
> Viscount Davignon is keen for "these dynamic businessmen" to succeed.

Such groups can sponsor the generation, evaluation, and dissemination of new development ideas, but they should avoid being identified with one particular approach to development (as was the Club of Rome). They should support the generation of alternative approaches, public discussion of these, and, where possible, experimental evaluation. In fact, an association of corporations of different nations might well create an "International Institute of Economic Development," sponsor an international journal and conferences, and provide a Nobel-like prize for contributions to our knowledge and understanding of economic development.

Corporations, perhaps more than any other institution in our societies, are in a position to transcend narrow national interests, to assume a position of leadership in promoting an international approach to development, and to support a more equitable distribution of wealth among nations.

Conclusion

In this chapter we have considered what corporations can do in an economy that is shifting from being production based to being service based to help alleviate unemployment and secure their own futures.

First, we identified ways in which corporations that produce goods can diversify into services. We suggested that they can do so by offering services that (1) are required by them, (2) are required by users of their products, and (3) require the use of their products. For such services to be successful, they must either correct a deficiency in a service currently available, fill a service gap, or exploit an opportunity provided by a new product.

Second, we considered how a company can develop or redevelop products and production processes to better satisfy needs and desires in both LDCs and MDCs. There are growing needs in LDCs for productive equipment, facilities, distribution systems, and consumer goods that are better suited to conditions in LDCs than in MDCs. In contrast, with accelerated automation there are opportunities in MDCs for increasingly sophisticated production equipment and facilities and distribution systems. There are also opportunities for developing products that can be used effectively in the provision of services for which there is an increasing demand, for example, products used in health, education, and environmental protection.

Finally, we considered how corporations can increase their ability to compete and hence provide employment by improving the quality of work life they provide and by rationalizing their behavior. Three aspects of corporate behavior were considered: improvement of (1) the effectiveness of management, particularly its ability to learn and adapt, (2) intraorganizational interactions, and (3) interorganizational interactions. With respect to the last, improvements of corporate relations with labor and government and collaboration among corporations provide significant opportunities for increasing the competitive effectiveness of corporations.

In the next three chapters, we shall describe efforts by three corporations that typify successful adaptation to changing economic and cultural conditions.

7

Successful Transformations: Examples in Business and Government

In this chapter we present five examples in which four corporations and one government agency transformed themselves in ways proposed in Chapters Five and Six. We also describe a sixth example in which a private corporation was created to provide a desired service that government providers had ignored.

To keep our descriptions brief, much detail has been omitted. Although this robs the cases of realism, it better reveals their morals. Were it not for the fact that they are real, they might better be called fables.

Debureaucratizing and Demonopolizing
an Internal Source of Service

The need to improve the quality and efficiency of services exists *within* organizations as well as in the external markets they serve. Bureaucratic and monopolistic divisions provide many of the services used within organizations. These internal providers are often the only sources of services that other parts of the organization are permitted to use. For this reason, they tend to provide poor service at a high cost and be unresponsive to their users.

With only minor modifications, the proposals made in Chapter Five for debureaucratizing and demonopolizing gov-

ernment service agencies apply to service units within corporations or governments. These proposals are:

1. enabling external suppliers to compete for the right to pro-
    vide services normally provided exclusively by internal
    sources;
2. requiring internal consumers to pay for as many services
    they receive as possible and making such payments the only
    source of income to the server;
3. if consumers cannot pay for a service, subsidizing the con-
    sumers rather than the server;
4. allowing internal consumers to buy services from external
    sources even when internal sources are available and allow-
    ing internal service providers to sell their services exter-
    nally; and
5. where a service supplier must be sudsidized, doing so ac-
    cording to the quality and quantity of service provided.

The next example illustrates the application of some of these
principles to a corporation.

A major oil company was one of the largest private users
of computers in the United States. The amount it spent on
computers and computing was rapidly approaching the amount
it spent on people. Computing services were provided exclusively by a corporate computing center, and the corporation
covered the costs; internal users were not charged for the service. As a result, the demand for the service exceeded the center's capacity.

Because of the excess demand for its services, the computing center had to assign priorities to requests for work. Its
users complained about frequent delays and the poor quality
of work. Many of them unsuccessfully sought their own computing facilities. On the other hand, management of the corporate computing center complained about the large number of
unjustified and unreasonable requests for service and the pressures applied for assigning high priorities to work that was submitted.

Corporate management concerned about the rapid growth
of the center and complaints from its management and users

commissioned an external research organization to conduct a cost-benefit analysis of the center. After several months of work, the organization found that the center's benefits could not be measured. In desperation, the research team examined the principal assumptions on which its efforts to make such measurements were based. It ultimately focused on the assumption that a third party could make a better cost-benefit analysis of a service than its users could. The researchers denied this assumption and explored the consequences of doing so.

The result was an unconventional set of recommendations to corporate management in which the users determined the value of the service:

1. All internal users should pay for computing services at prices set by the corporate center, but they should be free to purchase the services from external providers.
2. The computing center should be required to fill all internal requests but be free to sell its services to external users.
3. The center's only income should come from fees collected for the services it provided. Unless it can support itself, it should be discontinued.

This, in effect, converted the computing center into a profit unit competing in an open market.

These recommendations were accepted and implemented. In less than a year, the number of computers in the corporate center was reduced by about a third, but the center continued to provide virtually all the computing services required by the corporation. There was very little use of external sources. Furthermore, the center found that requests for service were more reasonable, and the corporate users found the services more satisfactory. In addition, a large portion of the center's services was sold to external users, and the center made a substantial profit. The total output of the center decreased, but the amount of useful output increased. In time the center grew larger than its original size, but it continued to operate profitably and to provide services that were valued by both its internal and external users.

The idea of converting an internal service center into a

profit center that competes against external suppliers has been generalized into what is called a "multidimensional organization" (Ackoff, 1981, chap. 7). In this type of organization every unit—service, line, or administrative—is a profit center. In effect, the corporation is converted from a centrally planned economy into one that is free. Every unit must justify itself by providing customers with value for money. If it fails to do so, it goes out of business.

Demonopolizing a Government Service

Monopolistic providers of service tend to be insensitive to the unfilled needs and desires of their users and employees. This often provides an opportunity for creating a superior competitive service. The competition provided the U.S. Postal Service by Federal Express is a case in point. Not only did Federal Express provide a needed but unavailable service, but it forced the Postal Service to do the same. The following case describes a similar situation in prerevolutionary Iran.

An Iranian Bank. Before the development of Bank-Saderat Iran (the Export Bank of Iran), the Iranian government controlled the country's banking industry. As a result, the banking system had relatively few branches, and these served primarily the needs of large customers in urban areas. The needs of smaller customers, especially those in rural areas, were ignored.

The Bank-Saderat Iran was privately developed to provide high-quality services to small depositors at a low cost. A key concept in the institution's development was service. At the same time, the new bank was committed to maintaining low overhead. It was designed to be sensitive and responsive to customers and to provide services that the government bank could not because of its organization.

The bank developed a decentralized structure with branches in urban neighborhoods and villages, and each branch was organized as a profit center. The basic organizational unit was a two-person team responsible for all bank functions, from opening new accounts to making loans. Small branches consisted of one team; larger branches, of two or more. The team members were recent high school graduates and had received six months of training. They were trained to think of themselves as bankers, not clerks. Each team consisted of a more experienced senior member and a junior apprentice. In time, the junior members became senior members and managed teams in branches of their own.

Each month every branch prepared a profit statement and its own balance sheet. This provided a strong incentive for keeping branch overhead low. Reduction of overhead was facilitated by a no-frills policy. The luxurious appointments normally found in most banks were forgone, and all employees, including the president, wore the same type of uniform.

To create a strong service orientation, team members were recruited from the neighborhoods and villages their branches served. They knew many of their customers personally and were sensitive to their needs.

The banks also met the needs of customers by using some all-female teams. In many parts of Iran, religious beliefs and social norms forbid women and men from interacting in public, even for business reasons. Women, therefore, will not go to branches staffed by men. Consequently, women bankers brought a previously unserved group of customers into the bank. Finally, mobile banks, similar to bookmobiles, were used to reach the smallest villages.

The bank grew rapidly and soon had more than 5,000 branches in Iran and Europe. In addition, it prompted the creation of other private banks in Iran.

Iranian Government's Health Services. A government's monopolistic service agency can be demonopolized by providing competing sources of service, even if these sources are government agencies themselves. This was done to the health services provided by the government in prerevolutionary Iran. These services were redesigned by the Industrial Management Institute in Teheran.

Traditional ways of providing health care, including those using third-party payments to private providers, were too expensive in Iran. In addition, the vastness of the country and the unwillingness of doctors to go to remote regions resulted in an inequitable distribution of health services. The redesigned system provided quality health care throughout the country.

In most large, public health care systems, supporting funds are distributed from the top down and the services are provided locally. However, although health care facilities were built in each Iranian province with government funds, they had to earn their income. This was done through a voucher system. Funds were distributed to the provinces on a per capita basis. The provinces, in turn, issued vouchers that could be redeemed at the government health care centers or at competing private providers. If the entire sum allocated each year to a province was not used for individual patient care, the surplus could be used for public health and environmental programs. This enabled the provinces to improve the quality of life.

Each provincial health care center determined its own design, setting up only those facilities and services that it could justify economically. However, it arranged with other centers to provide those services that it could not afford itself. It also provided its patients with transportation to these centers. In addition, jointly supported facilities were quite common, and were used for services that either were not in great demand or required scarce skills.

It was necessary to attract doctors to some remote facilities. An incentive plan was developed that paid doctors a base salary plus a fee for service. This fee was set for each province to reflect its remoteness and living conditions. Therefore, doctors working in extremely remote areas under very poor living conditions had very high incomes. This incentive system attracted doctors from developed urban areas to previously unserved areas.

By subsidizing demand through a voucher system, health services became more consumer oriented and flexible than they had been when provided by the government monopoly. Vouchers enabled those wanting health care to seek the best quality of service from a number of competitive sources. Moreover, the system enlarged the concept of health care itself by encouraging the use of surplus funds to establish preventive and educational health programs.

This health care system was one of very few government services not significantly changed in Iran after its revolution.

Giving a Service Provider Customer Feedback

Today's Man is a chain of men's clothing stores in the Philadelphia area. It grew from a pipe-rack store in a low-rent district that offered discount prices to four modern stores, one in the main shopping area of downtown Philadelphia and three in large, modern shopping malls in the suburbs. These stores offer a very large selection of men's clothing of medium and high quality at discount prices.

Although the chain has done reasonably well, it has failed to attract the kind of clientele its management has sought: upwardly mobile professionals and businessmen. Its customers were drawn primarily by the chain's prices, particularly during its frequent sales, and they displayed little loyalty to the stores. Market research revealed that the stores did not project the image that their owner and managers desired. Several efforts to rectify this through advertising had failed.

The chain's management approached the Busch Center of The Wharton School for help in finding a way to attract the type of customer it wanted. The experts in marketing and advertising who had previously been consulted had not succeeded. Then who could? Why not those whom the stores were trying to attract?

A sample of fifteen target customers was selected and brought to Busch Center to design their ideal men's clothing store. The top three executives of the chain were included but their affiliation was not revealed. The customers were told that there were no constraints other than that the stores had to be technologically feasible and capable of surviving in the current retail environment. The group was divided into two subgroups, each working independently.

Late in the day, the subgroups came together to present and discuss their designs. After the few minor differences between their designs were resolved, the identities of the sponsor and the attending managers were revealed. Then the differences between the design produced and the stores in the chain were discussed openly.

There were many important differences between the idealized store and Today's Man. These differences prompted the following suggestions:

1. Most important, the stores should not deliver a message of "quality at a low price" but "more quality for the money." The fifteen target customers said they decided how much to spend for the clothing they wanted before they shopped for it. Then they looked for the highest quality they could find at that price. They did not fix quality and try to minimize price.
2. The stores should offer only two sales per year, before summer and winter at the same times every year. Regular customers should be given an opportunity to make purchases before the sale is opened to the public.
3. The store should have a "clubby" atmosphere, intimate and affording some privacy to shoppers.
4. Sales personnel should be available on call but never apply pressure to customers.
5. Informative labeling should be on all articles. It should be accessible and easy to read and understand.
6. Rapid and free alterations should be provided.
7. A women's department should not be included, but there should be a place for women accompanying men to wait in comfort and be available for consultation.
8. People passing the store should not be able to see shoppers, but they should be able to get an impression of the content and size of the store.

The managers of the chain have been implementing a number of these features and report a noticeable improvement in the customer mix. They are now beginning to reach their target audience.

Intercorporate Collaboration

There are many things that a corporation acting alone cannot do to adapt to or modify its changing environment.

However, they can be done by several corporations working together. The following example of such collaboration is unusual because of its international character and what stimulated it.

An American industrial equipment company was in very serious financial trouble a short time ago. In an effort to avoid bankruptcy, the company's board acquired a new chief executive. Under his inspiring leadership, a participative planning process (like that used at Super Fresh) was initiated at the corporate and divisional levels. This process was initially directed at securing corporate survival, then revitalization, and eventually development.

One division of the company was particularly threatened. The industry of which it is a part is dominated by two giants, one U.S.-based and the other Japan-based. The Japanese firm has successfully invaded U.S., European, and other markets by introducing the most attractive part of its comprehensive product line—high-quality, high-volume, low-cost products. It obtained distribution for these products through dealers who handled the products of manufacturers of partial lines of equipment. The division of the American manufacturer tried to maintain sales volume or prevent erosion of their market share during the recession by meeting the Japanese firm's prices, even when doing so involved selling at a loss. This contributed significantly to the company's financial crisis.

Once the Japanese company had obtained a foothold in the marketplace, it began to increase the number of products available to its distributors. This threatened to push non-full-line manufacturers out of several distribution systems.

The American manufacturer determined that it could not stem the Japanese tide alone. Most other non-full-line construction equipment manufacturing companies faced the same prospects. To resolve this dilemma, the managers prepared a design of an idealized construction equipment company that they believed would be able to compete effectively against the two large competitors worldwide. Once this design was completed, the managers asked: What combination of existing companies, whatever their national base, would most closely approximate their idealized company? They identified four companies besides their own: three European firms and one Asian.

The possibility of combining these five companies into a joint venture seemed very remote. Nevertheless, management felt they had nothing to lose by trying. They approached the first European conglomerate, which they knew had only recently refused to sell the company they needed to several prospective buyers. They presented their analysis of the competitive situation and their proposed design. The conglomerate's management was impressed, agreed with their conclusions, and offered them the company. The sale was consummated in a very short time.

When the second European corporation was approached with the analysis and design, it too showed interest. It agreed to explore the proposed joint venture. A team of ten managers was formed, five from the American firm and five from the European. The presidents of the companies and senior managers of marketing, manufacturing, engineering, and finance from each were included. This group prepared a more detailed idealized design than the one already prepared by the American firm. It took into account the characteristics of the collaborating companies.

At this writing, a realizable version of the idealized design and plans for its implementation are almost complete. The joint design effort has brought the managers of the companies close together—in fact, they have become a very effective team. All are deeply committed to implementing their design. No disagreement arose during the design and planning process that could not be resolved to their complete satisfaction.

The design and plan of the joint venture will be submitted to the boards of the two companies while this book is in press. All who have been involved in the plan's preparation expect the plan to be accepted and the joint venture to be launched early in 1985.

Intracorporate Collaboration

Conflicts within corporations, particularly between labor and management, are often more intense than conflicts between corporations. Because internal conflict is a major obstacle to the ability of a corporation to compete effectively, labor-management collaboration is becoming more common. Since many of these collaborations are prompted by crises, they tend to have short lives. When the crisis is over, cooperation is often replaced by conflict. It is difficult to institutionalize such cooperation. It is not easy to change a corporate culture, because a complete transformation in the attitudes and behavior of labor and management is required. Making both parties commit themselves to cooperation is difficult, but it has been done. The following is a case in point.

Alcoa's Tennessee Operations (ATO) is the largest and oldest of Alcoa's installations in the United States. It consists of a smelter, two rolling mills, and a number of supporting facilities. The cost and quality of ATO's products deteriorated significantly after World War II, and the division had not performed well for many years. As a result, corporate headquarters decided in 1979 to phase out part of the division over the next five years.

A new operations manager was brought in shortly thereafter. He saw his task, similar to that of officiating at a wake, as hardly challenging. Therefore, he decided to use the time available to try to save the life of the condemned operations. Since he had virtually no capital for improving either the plant or its equipment and only very limited funds for maintenance, he found it difficult to determine which aspects of the operations he could make viable. He decided to try to find one through planning.

He persuaded corporate headquarters to allow him to hire a university-based planning group. In the first stage of this planning effort, ATO's situation was analyzed in depth. This analysis revealed that even with unlimited funds, it would be difficult to save the operations unless the productivity and product quality improved significantly.

The operations had a long history of labor-management hostility. The hourly workers were organized by Local 309 of the United Steel Workers of America. They were among the highest-paid production workers in the country and by far the highest in eastern Tennessee. Nevertheless, interviews revealed that most workers dreaded coming to work; the only reason they came was for the pay. They held management responsible for this sorry state of affairs, because they felt abused and exploited by management, which they saw as unconcerned with their working conditions and welfare.

Therefore, it became apparent to planners that unless labor-management relations were significantly improved, there was no hope of revitalizing the operations. However, management seriously doubted that the longstanding hostility with labor could be changed. Each side saw the other as intransigent. Nevertheless, top management saw no harm in trying to break the deadlock.

The university-based group made contact with the local's leadership, shared with them its analysis of ATO's situation, and proposed a meeting between them and management to explore the possibility of a cooperative effort to save the operations. This proposal was accepted but with great skepticism.

The meeting was held off-site in November 1980. It produced an agreement to encourage the labor and management groups in each department and at every level of the operation to organize. These groups were to be free to work on any problems agreed to by both parties. They were also encouraged to implement any solutions accepted by both sides as long as their solutions did not affect other organizational units and they had the resources required. If other units would be affected, the affected units would have to approve the solution before it could be implemented. If additional resources were needed, a request for them could be addressed to and processed by the lowest level of management that had access to the resources required.

This effort came to be known as the Trust and Cooperation (T&C) Program. Eighteen months after its initiation, an analysis revealed that most problems involved the hourly workers' quality of work life. Nevertheless, by the end of the second year, ATO's performance had improved in the following ways: (1) the grievance meeting rate had dropped by 70 percent, (2) the time-off disciplinary rate had dropped by 90 percent, (3) some customers felt product quality was the best in the country, (4) cost savings for the first half of 1982 were up by 20 percent compared with 1981, much of it attributable to the

T&C Program, and perhaps most significantly, (5) obstructions to change directed at improving the quality and quantity of product were considerably reduced.

These results led to a change in the attitude of corporate headquarters. On November 23, 1983, Alcoa announced a $250 million modernization plan for ATO. The president of Alcoa, Fred Fetterolf, said: "I can assure you this day would not have happened four years ago. It is happening now because of our increased confidence in the ability and willingness of Tennessee Alcoans to work together, adapt, and make it happen." The relationships between managers, union officials, and workers have gone through a profound transformation. Friendships have developed; mutual respect and understanding have grown; suspicion of the other has significantly decreased. The ability of labor and management to work things out cooperatively and their confidence in this ability have increased dramatically. Much remains to be done; for example, a significant portion of the employees, both labor and management, have yet to participate in the program. However, there is a strong conviction that what needs to be done will be.

Conclusion

These cases are intended to show that the types of changes in government and corporations that we suggested in Chapters Five and Six can be carried out. Some of these changes were stimulated by crises, but not all of them. In some cases, a realization of the magnitude of the changes occurring in the environment is sufficient to instigate change. An organization can become aware of the implications of environmental changes by carrying out a "reference projection." This is a projected future of the organization based on two (presumably false) assumptions: first, that the organization will not change any of its current policies and practices, and second, that the environment will continue to change but only in expected ways. Under these assumptions, every organization would destroy itself because it would not adapt to even the expected changes. (For details, see Ackoff, 1981, chap. 4.)

Such an exercise reveals the Achilles' heel of an organization and the crises that it will eventually face if it does not change. It was just such a projection that revealed to the American equipment manufacturer that it would not survive as an independent manufacturer. The same kind of projection revealed to Alcoa's Tennessee Operations that it would not survive without a marked increase in labor's productivity. Such a revelation is often enough to stimulate the kinds of changes we have proposed.

8

Returning
a Troubled Business
to Profitability:
Case Study of Super Fresh

In Chapter Six we argued that productivity and the quality of work in corporations can be significantly improved by converting the usual adversarial relationship between labor and management into a cooperative one. In addition, we argued that this is best done by having all the stakeholders participate in the design of the cooperative relationship. The case presented here, that of the supermarket chain Super Fresh, demonstrates that this is possible. Moreover, it shows it can be done even in a business that is dead, not merely dying. The Super Fresh experience has an added significance: It involves an enterprise engaged not in production but in providing services.

The Great Atlantic & Pacific Tea Company (A&P) had been in trouble since the early 1970s. Because of mounting losses, management and ownership had changed several times during that decade. The number of stores had been cut from about 3,500 in 1974 to 1,000 in March 1982.

In the Philadelphia metropolitan area, the company closed about 60 of its 110 stores in two years, 40 of these early in 1982. The company blamed the high cost of labor and the union that represented its employees, Locals 56 and 1357 of the United Food and Commercial Workers (UFCW). Despite very high sales per employee compared with the rest of the industry, A&P's labor cost was much higher than average: 15 percent of operating revenues compared with 10 percent for the industry as a whole.

Because of seniority clauses in the labor contracts, the layoffs resulting from store closings primarily affected part-time, young, and low-paid workers. The average length of service of A&P's employees was twice that of other supermarket chains.

Early in 1982, Local 1357, greatly concerned about the imminent closing of A&P's stores in the Philadelphia area, consulted the Busch Center of The Wharton School of the University of Pennsylvania. Through the discussions that followed, it became clear that jobs could not be saved without redefining the role of the union. Once this was accepted, the union decided to try to organize its members to buy and operate some of the stores that A&P was about to close. It proposed buying two stores early in March 1982 and called on its members for financial support. In the next two weeks, 600 members pledged $5,000 each. The problem the union then had to confront was how to succeed where the company had failed.

The union, unlike A&P's management, believed that the workers knew how to operate supermarkets successfully. Their knowledge had never been tapped by management, but the union decided to do so. It formed teams of workers and gave them the task of designing a new way of organizing a supermarket and managing it themselves. It also saw the necessity and accepted the responsibility of retraining workers who would be involved in managing and operating the new stores.

The offer made by former employees to purchase two stores led A&P's management to rethink its position and consider alternatives to further store closings. This, in turn, induced the union, with the help of its consultants, to develop a proposal that came to be known as the Quality of Work Life Plan. Using this plan as a starting point, negotiations between the union and management began.

The negotiations were cooperative, not adversarial. The common objective of keeping the stores open dominated the discussions. The outcome was reported in *Business Week* ("Worker Ownership May Save Some A&Ps," 1981, pp. 44-45) as follows:

> A&P reached agreement in May [1982] with Locals 1357 and 56 of the United Food and Commercial Workers (UFCW). But the plan's innovative nature became clearer in mid June as both sides met to tie down details. The Locals accepted shorter vacations and pay cuts of up to $2 an hour in return for an A&P promise to reopen 20 stores and give workers a chance to buy as many as four others. A&P also agreed to set up quality circles, or committees of workers and supervisors, at the 20 stores to get workers' ideas on improving performance. . . . Wendell W. Young, Local 1357's president, says the UFCW agreed to try to hold labor costs at the 20 stores to 10% of operating revenues. In recent years, these costs had risen to 14.9%.
>
> In exchange, the workers in each store will get 1% of gross sales. This share will be reduced if labor costs exceed 10% of revenues and will be increased if they fall below 9%. Some 40% to 50% of the gross sales fund will go for bonuses, and the rest will go into a fund to help workers buy closed stores. . . .
>
> If the plan works, more than 1,000 laid-off workers could regain their jobs. Local 1357 has lost about 5,000 members since 1976 because of closings of grocery and nonfood stores. The test will be whether labor-management cooperation and the productivity-incentive plan can make the reopened stores profitable in a fiercely competitive market. . . .
>
> Of the 24 stores involved in the UFCW agreement, 20 will operate under a new A&P subsidiary named Super Fresh Food Markets. Workers have already pledged $3 million to buy at least three of the other stores and have an option to buy the fourth. . . .

In the Philadelphia plan, supermarket clerks will take a 20% pay cut, to $8 an hour, and meatcutters will take a 14.7% cut, to $10.50. Paid vacations are reduced from four weeks after 20 years' service to one week, and workers will receive only time-and-a-half pay for Sunday work, instead of double time. Wages will increase by $1 per hour annually in the first two years of the three-year pact, and workers will receive the incentive bonuses on top of that. The UFCW locals also agree to radical seniority changes. If one of the new Super Fresh stores closes, its employees would not be able, as before, to "bump" union members in another A&P supermarket in the region.

The Busch Center was selected to work with the company and the locals to help develop their quality-of-work-life (QWL) program. By mid June three design teams were formed. These included workers from every level, from the president of Super Fresh to part-time clerks. The first Super Fresh markets opened in mid July 1982.

To prepare its members for the new and different work environment, Locals 56 and 1357 prepared a handbook, *Quality of Work Life*, which we reproduce here in its entirety.

Dear Super Fresh Member:

We are happy to give you this Quality of Work Life handbook. It is the result of a long process of development that started with the historic creation of Super Fresh.

A committee of employees, union leaders, and Super Fresh management prepared this document in an effort to create a management style suited to this new venture.

By following this guide, it is our hope that the working conditions in your store will continually improve. Of course, we are all aware that the profitability of your store can also grow as we learn to work together.

It is up to you, with your active participation to breathe life into this unique concept.

We are looking forward to a strong working relationship

with you so that we will all achieve the successes we know can
be ours.

s/s LEO CINAGLIA
President, UFCW Local 56

s/s WENDELL W. YOUNG, III
President, UFCW Local 1357

s/s/ GERALD L. GOOD
President, Super Fresh Markets, Inc.

I. MISSION

To create a viable shopping environment that provides
the customer with a consistent and satisfying shopping experience on a day-to-day basis.

To do this effectively Super Fresh will pursue the following three interrelated objectives:

- Provide a quality product; a courteous, pleasant, and helpful shopping environment; and a pricing structure which represents value to the customer.
- Create a unique, positive experience for employees to increase their quality of working life through helping design
their future as employees and the future of the company.
- Generate a new model that demonstrates a successful and
profitable operation of a volume-oriented business.

Super Fresh Food Markets will create a new working
style and environment for the food retail business that will encourage a quality of work life where the employees have the desire and the ability to improve themselves as well as the business
they are in. This environment will be enhanced by opportunities
for employees: participation in an investment/incentive fund;
participation in decisions that affect them; to continuously
learn and grow in their jobs. This will give them a sense of ownership, not only in the individual store, but in the company as a

whole. Super Fresh and the Unions will have a relationship that is trusting and cooperative so that they work together for the benefit of each other. Super Fresh will be recognized within the food retailing industry and within each community served by Super Fresh as the model which others try to emulate. At the same time Super Fresh will, by its performance, redefine upwardly the industry's standard of profit.

II. SPECIFICATIONS

1. General
   1.1. The organizational design will be based on the criteria of incorporating the advantages of operating an individual autonomous supermarket along with the advantages of the synergistic effects of combining the stores into a corporation.
   1.2. The organization will operate with as few management levels as possible.
   1.3. Decisions will be made at the lowest possible level where participation will be reflected by authority and responsibility.
   1.4. The employees, called associates, will have access to information about their work and the corporation which will allow for meaningful input to decisions.
   1.5. The organization will be capable of functional flexibility. Emphasis will be placed on organizational learning and adaptability.
   1.6. The relationship between Super Fresh and the Union will be cooperative; they will assist each other in obtaining mutual objectives.
   1.7. The organization is to be so constructed that it is assured of being:
      • Economically viable.
      • Technologically feasible.
      • Able to adapt to the changing needs of its environment and its members.
      • Able to encourage a quality of work life (QWL)

where the associates have both the *desire* and *ability* to improve themselves and the company with which they are associated.

1.8. Each store is the output unit of Super Fresh, and can be viewed as a subsidiary of Super Fresh, using the services provided by Super Fresh for its advantage. These individual stores' performances will be measured by three factors:
- Gross sales.
- Labor ratio (percentage of gross sales).
- Contribution to Super Fresh (dollars and percentage of sales).

1.9. The image of Super Fresh should reflect, among other things, the unique organizational design of associate, union, and management cooperativeness.

2. *Output*

Super Fresh will constantly pursue the following objectives:
- Loyal customers.
- Satisfied employees.
- Adequate return on investment.

2.1. *Products*

A good selection of prepackaged, processed, and prepared products should be provided.
- Items offered for sale by each store will be tailored to the customers' needs within each community served by a store.
- Stores will strive to develop a one-stop food service for its customers.
- Stores will not be limited to food items and may sell nonfood items as well.

2.2. *Services*

There will be a variety of convenience services available for customers. These will include:
- Check cashing.
- Customer service center.
- Customer special orders.
- Customer education.

2. *Processes*

The following processes will transform inputs to outputs.

3.1. The following processes will be performed by the organization at the corporate level:
- Employee development.
- Financial planning and control, including asset control, capital investment, etc.
- Human resource management.
- Procurement and distribution.
- Marketing.
- Policy setting.
- Performance monitoring.
- Store selection and property management.
- Union-Management relationship (including collective bargaining).

3.2. The following processes will be performed by the organization at the store level:
- Each department should manage its own processes, such as selecting, ordering, storing, displaying.
- Customer handling and relations.
- Cleaning.
- Scheduling/development.
- Risk management.
- Human resources management.
- Cash and asset control.
- Union, store management, and associate relationships (grievances).
- Community relationships.

4. *Input*

4.1. *Money*

The capital investment will be provided by A&P. Super Fresh Corporation will generate the working capital needed for the successful operation of the Corporation. A&P's assistance in obtaining business credit will be requested whenever need arises. The President will negotiate to retain a percentage of the contribution (profit) for reinvestment in Super Fresh, for example, modernization and expansion.

4.2. *Knowledge*

Associates will be taught to be proficient in their jobs and will also be exposed to the total supermarket operation. The knowledge requirement of the company will be principally provided internally by the associates.

4.3. *People*

Personnel will be selected to facilitate the attainment of the Super Fresh mission.

4.4. *Facilities*

Facilities for the stores will be designed to suit specific locations. Equipment for the stores will be standardized for easier maintenance and modifications.

4.5. *Inventory*

Super Fresh will obtain inventory from A&P on a competitive basis. Super Fresh will also obtain inventory locally when needed.

5. *Environment*

Super Fresh will create working relationships with the following stakeholders:

- Associates.
- Customers.
- Community at large.
- Unions.
- Suppliers.
- Creditors.
- Service vendors.
- Former A&P employees.
- A&P.

III. ORGANIZATIONAL DESIGN

6. *Overview*

Super Fresh will be organized as a two/three-level structure. The first level will be that of the corporation itself, which will incorporate five different dimensions:

- Output Units (stores).
- Input Units (service functions).
- Environmental Unit (marketing/advocacy).
- Planning Boards (policy-making bodies).
- Management Support System (control).

The second level will be the internal structure of the store itself, which will be organized along the same concept as the corporation, having the five dimensions of the larger system.

- Output Units (departments).
- Input Units (front end, receiving).
- Environmental Unit (local business development and advocacy).
- Planning Boards (policy-making bodies).
- Management Support System (control).

As Super Fresh increases the number of stores it operates, a three-level structure will be created that groups the stores into regional units.

6.1. *Output Units.* Achievement of the organizational ends and objectives (outputs) will be the responsibility of the output units (stores) of the system. The other units are created in order to facilitate the operation of these units. These units will be self-sufficient and autonomous to the degree that the integrity of the whole system is not compromised.

6.2. *Input Units.* Inputs are the services required to support the output units. Because of economies of scale, technology and geographic dispersion inputs can best be realized at the corporate level. These units will also be semiautonomous.

6.3. *Environmental Units.* The interaction of the system with its environment is facilitated by the environmental units. The two main functions of these units are marketing and advocacy, that is, attracting the customers, making contact with the external stakeholders, and advocating their point of view within the system.

6.4. *Planning Board.* Planning is a process that provides the overall coordinating and integrating function for the input, output, and environmental units. Planning boards are the main policy-making body of the organization and at all levels serve as the vehicle for the participative management style of Super Fresh. This enables the information, judgments, and concerns of subordinates to influence the decisions that affect them. One of the key functions of the planning boards is to constantly reassess the progress the corporation, store, or department is making toward its goals (via feedback from the management support system) and to chart new objectives when necessary. Planning at the store level is directed at those matters affecting the store. Planning affecting more than one store is done at the corporate level.

6.5. *Management Support Systems.* The management support system is responsible for the comparison of the actual outcomes versus expected outcomes on the plans and policies set by the planning boards. This provides the means for learning and adaptation.

7. *Components of the System*

7.1. *Stores* (Output Units)

7.1.1. The stores will produce the outputs of Super Fresh. Therefore, those activities which are directly compatible with the mission of the "whole," and are necessary for the production of outputs will be considered in this dimension.

7.1.2. Each store will be responsible for the management of its resources and will have an organizational structure very similar to the larger system of which it is part.

7.1.3. Each store will operate as a semiautono-

mous performance center. Financial contributions of each store to Super Fresh will
reflect the sales minus direct costs, but corporate indirect costs will not be charged.

7.1.4. Each store will be allowed to retain a percentage of its contributions above a minimum level determined by the corporate
planning board. These funds will be used
for internal development and local business
development by the store consistent with
corporate board policies.

7.1.5. Each store will be responsible for making
those decisions which affect only its operations. Decisions which impact on other
stores and the corporation as a whole will
be made at the corporate level with participation from the Store Director.

7.1.6. Each Store Director will report directly to
the Office of the President of Super Fresh.

7.1.7. Each store and department will have a planning board of its own.

7.1.8. At the store level each output department
will be headed by a manager who reports
directly to the Store Director. The output
departments will be as follows:
• Grocery.
• Meat.
• Produce.
• Deli/Bakery.

7.1.9. The Store Director will be responsible for
general store orientation for all new associates. This orientation will be assessed by
the department managers.

7.1.10. The Store Directors in conjunction with
department managers will develop cross-
departmental familiarization programs
which will be assessed by the Store Director and those who participate in the programs.

7.2. *Support Services* (Input Units)

7.2.1. The nature and the role of the input units will be to provide the stores and the "whole" with the inputs and services required.

7.2.2. Only direct costs of work performed by outside units will be charged to the stores. The indirect costs of supplying the services will not be charged to the stores.

7.2.3. There will be a pilot study to compare the system defined in 7.2.2. with the use of competitors in providing support services.

7.2.4. The following functional service areas will be grouped into units, each of which will report directly to the Office of the President.

- Human Resources:
  Personnel, training, labor relations, benefit administration, associate education.
- Finance and Information Services:
  Accounting, investment services, billing, and banking.
- Retail Operations:
  Store services including maintenance.
- Distribution:
  Centralized warehousing, transport, and delivery.
- Risk Management:
  Prevention of associate and customer accidents, fire, and loss.

7.2.5. The input units will be evaluated by the quality and the effectiveness of the services provided to the output units.

7.2.6. At the store level the following input units will provide services to the departments:

- Front End.
- Receiving.

7.2.7. Each input unit will have a planning board of its own.

7.3. *Marketing/Advocacy* (Environmental Unit)

7.3.1. The marketing unit will be responsible for constant scanning and interaction with the external environment and stakeholders (customers, vendors, community, neighborhood, A&P, etc.).

7.3.2. Marketing services will provide:
- Market intelligence (new products, packaging).
- Suggested product mix (see Section 8.1).
- Suggested retail price (see Section 8.1).
- Area advertising.
- Setup and merchandising consulting services.

7.3.3. The advocacy effort will consist of sensing the situation in the environment and supplying the information to the planning boards. It will assist the decision-making process. Once decisions are made, the new goals will be given to the management support system for monitoring. Therefore, the advocacy interlinked with the planning boards and the management support systems (control) will constitute the mechanisms for learning and adaptation.

7.3.4. The marketing unit will report directly to the President.

7.3.5. The marketing unit will be an overhead center; however, stores will not be charged directly for its services.

7.3.6. Each store will also develop a method of consistently assessing the needs of the customers and of the neighborhood in order to be responsive to those needs. The Store Director will be responsible for marketing activities, including among others, review of customer feedback forms, keeping a file of products requested by customers, recognizing special customers, and furthering community relations.

7.4. *Planning Boards*

7.4.1. There will be planning boards at all levels, including the corporation as a whole, support service units, and stores.

7.4.2. In general, each board will consist of (1) the manager of the unit whose board it is, (2) his/her immediate superior, (3) his/her immediate subordinates, and (4) representatives of the associates on higher boards. The specific membership will be identified in Sections 7.4.11 through 7.4.15.

7.4.3. The planning boards will be engaged in continuous interactive planning and research to redesign the system as needed.

7.4.4. The planning boards will be policy-making bodies and not merely advisory committees; however, executive decisions will be left to the respective managers.

7.4.5. Organizational strategies, policies, and procedure will be formulated by the planning boards.

7.4.6. The planning boards will explicitly specify the objectives and consequences of the plans and policies designed by the board. These objectives and their attainment will be assessed on a regular basis by the management support system.

7.4.7. The planning boards will utilize the information generated by all the units.

7.4.8. Decisions will be made by a consensus of the board members. If consensus cannot be reached as to a course of action, the board will resolve the differences by research and experimentation by special project committees.

7.4.9. Those holding management positions will

be appointed by their immediate higher-level manager; however, they will have to maintain the confidence of their respective planning boards.

7.4.10. The corporate planning board will make available through Human Resources information and sources on internal and external training on the operation of the food retailing business and its environment. This information will be available to all associates.

7.4.11. At the corporate level the board will meet on a regular basis and will have the following members:

- The President of Super Fresh.
- The Director of each store.
- Representatives of associates-at-large selected by store planning boards.
- The Support Service and the Marketing Unit Directors.
- The Presidents of the two Unions.
- The responsible manager of A&P or his/her representative.
- External stakeholders, if the issue warrants it.

7.4.12. When the number of stores increases, the corporate board will be divided into subcorporate boards, meeting regionally. No more than fifteen stores will be included in a subcorporate board. The subcorporate board will have the following members:

- The Vice President of Retail Operations (representing the President) and his/her assistants (who may function as regional managers).
- The Director of each store (maximum 15).

- An associate from each of the stores to be chosen by each store planning board on a rotational basis.
- The Support Services and the Marketing Unit Directors.
- The representatives of the two Unions' management.

7.4.13. Coordination of the subcorporate boards will be done in a special meeting of the corporate planning board at which time an overall corporate plan will be formulated. The following will attend:
- The President.
- The Vice President of Retail Operations and his/her regional assistants.
- One store Director and one associate from each region selected by the subcorporate planning board on a rotational basis.
- Support Services and Marketing Directors.
- The Presidents of each of the two Unions or their representatives.
- A responsible manager of A&P or his/her representative.

7.4.14. At the store level the board will meet on a regular basis and will have the following members:
- The Store Director and his/her assistants.
- The Manager of each department and an associate to be chosen by the department planning board:
  - Grocery.
  - Meat.
  - Produce.
  - Deli/Bakery.
- The Front End Manager and a cashier.
- The representatives of the two Unions.

- A representative of the President of Super Fresh.

7.4.15. At the department level the board will meet on a regular basis and will include all the associates of that department.

7.5. *Management Support System* (Control)

7.5.1. The management support system will evaluate the degree to which the goals and objectives have actually been realized, and with what efficiency and effectiveness. It will also identify areas of unsatisfactory performance for management attention and action where appropriate.

7.5.2. It will guide the efforts and actions of managers at all levels of the organization toward the achievement of organizational objectives. It is important to note that the management support system will constitute the learning process by generating positive and negative feedback and therefore positive and negative reinforcement.

7.5.3. The management support system will, on a continuous basis, monitor the following: Financial Performance, Quality of Work Life, and Customer Satisfaction. As in all other components this will be done at both the store and corporate level.

7.5.3.1. Financial control will refer to those efforts directed at controlling the financial resources and monitoring financial performance of the organization.

7.5.3.2. QWL control will refer to those efforts directed at controlling and monitoring the improvement of quality of work life.

7.5.3.3. Customer satisfaction will refer to those efforts directed at controlling the operations, specific tasks or activities of the organization which are directed at the customer.

7.5.4. A substantial portion of the planning activities of the organization will constitute an integral part of the control process. These efforts will provide the basis of the corporation's learning process as it will assess the actual outcome of the various actions taken by the planning boards.

7.5.5. The management support system directors will report to and will be evaluated by the President.

8. *Important Issues*

8.1. *Pricing and Product Mix Structures*

8.1.1. There will be a flexible and responsive pricing-product mix structure at the individual store level for maximum profitability.

8.1.2. There will be four categories involved in the product mix and pricing structure. These will be prepared by the Marketing Unit and presented to the Store as follows:

I. Mandatory prices, mandatory product mix.

II. Mandatory prices, choice of product mix.

III. Choice of prices, mandatory product mix.

IV. Choice of prices, choice of product mix.

		Mandatory	Choice
Pricing	Choice	III	IV
	Mandatory	I	II
		Mandatory	Choice
		Product Mix	

8.1.3. Presently the information system allows for categories I and II.
- Group I consists of mandatory products to be sold at mandatory retail price. These products will be solely supplied by Super Fresh via A&P or approved vendors and the stores will have to carry them.
- Group II consists of optional products to be sold at mandatory retail price. These products will be solely supplied by Super Fresh via A&P or approved vendors; however, the stores have the authority to order what is required to meet specific local needs.

8.1.4. Until the system is enlarged to accommodate groups III and IV each store will have a list of specific items for which the marketing department need only be informed of price changes. Price changes involving the remaining items require the approval of the marketing department.

8.2. *Incentive Systems*

8.2.1. Each store will contribute a percentage of its sales depending upon total labor cost percentage to an associate investment/incentive fund. The decisions regarding allocation, investment, and disbursement of this fund are the right of the associates. The Union will facilitate the forming of an advisory committee to make these decisions (outside the Super Fresh QWL effort).

8.2.2. Super Fresh will establish a management incentive fund in which each Store Director will participate. The incentive will be paid based on performance in the following areas:
- Sales.

- Employee satisfaction.
- Store contribution.

8.3. *Hiring*

    8.3.1. Former A&P employees will be given preference in hiring at the store level. Placement of these individuals will be done by a hiring committee made up of:

- The Director of Human Resources.
- The Vice Presidents of the two Unions.
- The Store Director will be consulted on the list of Departmental Managers being considered for his store.

This procedure will operate as long as there is a list of former A&P or Super Fresh employees.

8.4. *Promotion*

    8.4.1. Super Fresh will fill any position vacancy in the following order:

- Promote from within the unit (store or functional area).
- Recruit from within Super Fresh (across store or service units).
- Hire from list of former A&P or Super Fresh employees.
- Hire from outside.

8.5. *Selection of Store Directors*

    8.5.1. Store directors will be selected by the Vice President of Retail Operations in cooperation with Human Resources. Evaluation of present associates for the position of Store Director will be based upon:

- Performance.
- Store planning board recommendations.
- Corporate planning board review of candidates.
- Peer feedback.
- Customer relations.
- Managerial ability.

APPENDIX

A. The Approach

There are two conventional approaches to planning: the *reactive* and the *preactive*.

Reactive planning consists essentially of identifying deficiencies and designing separate projects to remove each. Unfortunately, the removal of a deficiency (getting rid of what we don't want) gives us no assurance of obtaining what we do want —for example, changing the TV channel when one obtains an undesirable program. Furthermore, this approach fails to recognize that the outcome produced by implementing a plan is *not* the sum of the separate effects of its parts, but a product of their interactions.

Preactive planning consists of predicting the future and preparing for it. Such planning can be no better than the predictions on which it is based and these are notoriously subject to significant error. Moreover, our preparations (and those of others) affect the future that has been predicted. Thus, accurate predictions presuppose knowledge of the preparations which, in turn, presuppose the predictions. This is a very vicious circle. Finally, all predictions are based on extrapolations from the past, but the further out the state we try to predict, the more it depends on what will be done and will happen between now and then.

Therefore, the Planning Team took the *interactive* approach to planning in which planning is taken to consist of *the design of a desirable future and the selection and invention of ways of bringing it about.* Such planning has two phases, *idealization* in which the design is prepared, and *realization* in which ways of bringing it about are selected or invented. The effort of the Planning Team was largely devoted to the first phase; now steps toward realization are occurring.

The design prepared is called "idealized" because it assumes the system or organization planned for has been wiped out; hence it "starts from scratch." Its product is that system or organization with which the designers would replace the existing system or organization *right now* if they were free to do so. The only constraints imposed on the design are that it be technologically feasible and capable of surviving in the same environment that the existing system or organization operates in. It need not be attainable, but it invariably turns out to be capable of being more closely approximated than one might suppose. Thus, it provides a target, a desired future, toward the approximate attainment of which the realization phase of planning is directed.

Since our concept of what is ideal changes over time—particularly with efforts to realize it—idealized designs are subject to continual improvements. The one developed by the Planning Team and presented here is not an exception. We expect it to be improved over time, especially as more people become involved with it.

The product of an idealized design is *not* an ideal or utopian system precisely because it can be improved. Rather, it is the best *ideal-seeking* system that its designers can conceive of at the time it is prepared. [The List of Planning Team Participants and Busch Center Participants is omitted here.]

We have reproduced this document because it exemplifies an effort to produce an adaptive-learning organization, one that can increase its productivity even in a rapidly changing environment. Concern with both productivity and quality of work life permeates every aspect of the design.

Now, what has happened to Super Fresh?

Super Fresh opened its twenty-ninth store in December 1982. Its original goal was to open twenty-four stores by that time. It sought to hire 2,000 workers by the end of the year; it actually hired 2,105. The new stores, in the same locations as previously unprofitable stores, established record sales and profits almost every week. In June 1983, A&P announced its first profitable quarter in two years.

9

Agenda
for Public Action

The measures for combating unemployment that we proposed
for corporations are easier to adopt than those we proposed
for governments. The pressure of competition and the bottom
line is usually enough to induce corporations to explore new directions. Governments have no competition and no bottom
line; they are unregulated, bureaucratic monopolies and, like all
such organizations, resist change even when it is urgently called
for because of changing conditions. Governments will certainly
resist our proposals, since the proposals would reduce the size
of many governmental departments and agencies, increase their
accountability, force them to compete, and impose a bottom
line. Thus, they would be threatened by the possibility of being
dismantled if they did not perform well.

Because corporations can make the changes we proposed
without governmental support or direct public involvement, and
because these changes are in corporations' best interests, some
of our suggestions are already being implemented and more will
be in the future. Nevertheless, government can increase the rate
of implementation. For example, if governments were to "pri-
vatize" portions of the public sector, corporations would move
into services much faster. Without privatization, it is not likely
that the private sector can do enough to reduce unemployment
significantly.

Government is unlikely to make the changes we have proposed unless it is pressured by the public. Therefore, it is unlikely that the unemployment problem will be treated effectively unless the public intervenes. Appealing to the public to intervene by devoting its time, energy, and material resources to reducing unemployment is, in effect, asking it to assume responsibility for the problem. If, in a democracy, ultimate power resides in the people, then ultimate responsibility does, too. What can the public do and how can it be induced to do it? We shall address these questions in this chapter.

The Public's Task

We have argued as follows:

1. there is a growing desire for services;
2. if this desire was translated into demand, enough employment could be created in the service sector to significantly reduce, if not eliminate, unemployment;
3. the conversion of a large portion of the desire for services into demand is unlikely to occur because of the current low quality and high cost of services;
4. these problems derive from the fact that most services are provided by bureaucratic monopolies in either government or the private sector; therefore,
5. the providers of services must be demonopolized and debureaucratized to solve the unemployment problem.

However, government is not likely to do this precisely because it is the largest, least regulated, most bureaucratic monopoly of all. Therefore, it is the responsibility of the public, the governed, to demonopolize and debureaucratize government by reclaiming its authority over it.

The public will not try to redo its government unless it has a common vision of the type of government it wants. We believe that in many MDCs, particularly in the United States, the public has such a vision, but it is vague. Abraham Lincoln specified its most general characteristic: that it be a "government of the people, by the people, for the people." We need not debate whether the government of the United States is of the people or for the people, because it clearly is not *by* the people.

It could be argued that when small communities were governed by town meetings, they were governed by the people, but those days are long gone. We live in an age of big, centralized, nonparticipative government. As E. S. Savas (1982, p. 8) observed, it did not start this way:

> Growth has not occurred uniformly at all levels of government. Federal expenditures have grown much more rapidly than non-federal ones, and state expenditures in turn have grown more rapidly than local ones; therefore the latter have been shrinking steadily in relative terms. This represents an increasing centralization of power at higher levels of government and, by contrast, a waning of local government.

In apparent contradiction to Savas, John Naisbitt (1982, p. 2) wrote:

> We are shifting from institutional help to more self-reliance in all aspects of our lives. We are discovering that the framework of representative democracy has become obsolete in an era of instantaneously shared information. We are giving up our dependence on hierarchical structures in favor of informal networks.

This contradiction is only apparent, not real. Governments are becoming more centralized, but an increasing number of people are trying to become less dependent on and regulated by them. The growth of the hidden economy reflects this. It is also reflected in what S. M. Miller and Donald Tomaskovic-Devey (1983) call "today's antibureaucratic, antigovernment, antipolitician ethos." They go on to observe:

> The participation/empowerment orientation is responsive to American values and desires in ways foreign to the bureaucratic welfare state. For

one of the great, continuing strengths and delights (as well as constraints) of American life is localism. The popular theme of empowerment enables neighborhoods and communities to determine organizational structures and to carry through the activities and programs that affect them. Models of service organization and delivery which emphasize local decision-making and democracy, the realization of the positive American ideas of community and liberty . . . should largely displace "Big State" welfare state/socialist models of centralized direction and heavy bureaucratic control. Enhancing freedom and autonomy are important American themes which progressives and liberals have underemphasized in recent years [pp. 152–153].

In recent years we have also tended to forget that the government of the United States has gone through a radical evolution since its establishment. When it was formed, the population of the country was just over two million. The largest city, New York, contained only slightly more than 30,000 people, and fewer than a dozen cities had more than 10,000 people. Government in North America began at the local level and gradually moved up, reducing power at the local level and thus acquiring its current hierarchical structure.

Most of even the smallest political units in the United States are now too large to be governed participatively. New York, Chicago, and Los Angeles contain more people than the United States did when its government was formed, but these cities still have only one level of government. The more we are governed by representatives and the lower the ratio of representatives to the represented, the more self-contained government becomes and the more it is separated from the governed.

Isn't it impossible for large groups of people to govern themselves? Doesn't self-government in a large society imply anarchy? Isn't representative government the only way to democracy in a large society? *No, there is another way.* It involves a conversion from representative democracy to participative democracy.

Before we consider the nature of a participative democ-

racy, recall the four ways of treating a problem specified in
Chapter Three:

1. absolution—ignoring it,
2. resolution—selecting a course of action that is good enough,
3. solution—selecting the best available course of action, and
4. dissolution—changing the system to eliminate the problem
    and to enable the system to do better in the future than
    the best it can do now.

Recall also that problem resolution involves a clinical approach based on common sense, qualitative judgment, and experience; problem solution involves a research approach based
on quantitative scientific methods; problem dissolution involves
the use of *design*.

The importance of design is made apparent when we consider the urging of people like Miller and Tomaskovic-Devey
(1983), who advocate turning more of government back to the
people but nevertheless recognize the need for a central government:

> National guidelines are necessary to prevent
> ethnic and social stratification and segregation, to
> promote equitable use of facilities, to guard against
> abuses, etc. But these are essentially monitoring
> roles rather than centralized construction and con-
> trol of services. Governments will have to learn
> how to monitor service delivery without overload-
> ing localities with rules and regulations. National
> standards are also needed for environmental, tax,
> and labor costs so that communities do not need to
> compete with each other for corporate leavings
> [pp. 154-155].

However, Miller and Tomaskovic-Devey leave vague the details
of how such a government would be structured and function.
No amount of urging is likely to move the public to adopt a
largely unspecified type of government. A *design* of the government to be sought is required.

What Kind of Design?

If we try to design a government that is politically feasible, it will not differ significantly from the government we have. Nothing inhibits innovation as much as preoccupation with feasibility. To avoid this constraint, we employ an *idealized design process* (Ackoff, 1981, chap. 6). In this process the designers assume that the system they want to change was completely destroyed last night, but its environment and members remain intact. Then they produce a conception of the system that they would most like to replace the destroyed system with *right now*, not at some future date. Therefore, the environment in which the proposed system would operate need not be forecast; it is the current environment. Nevertheless, assumptions about the future operating environment must, of course, enter into the design.

In conventional system design, estimates of a design's feasibility are usually inferred from estimates of the feasibility of its parts taken separately. Therefore, a design, like a chain, is taken to be no more feasible than its least feasible link. This inference is wrong. A design is not a chain. It is a *system* of decisions. Therefore, the design as a whole has properties that none of its parts have, and its parts acquire properties that they would not otherwise have. Therefore, it is possible to produce a feasible design none of whose parts, taken separately, are feasible. It is equally possible to have an infeasible design each of whose parts, taken separately, is feasible.

For example, the idealized redesign of Paris prepared in the 1970s (Ozbekhan, 1977) included a number of changes that, had they been proposed individually to the French government, would surely have been dismissed as infeasible. One was that the capital of France be moved out of Paris, and another was that Paris be made a self-governing open city not subject to the government of France. In view of the mission adopted for Paris, that it become the informal capital of the world, these two changes were seen not only as feasible but as absolutely necessary. For this reason the government of France has taken significant steps toward their realization.

When a preliminary version of the idealized design of the National Scientific Communication and Technology Transfer System (Ackoff and others, 1976) was presented to a large group of its stakeholders for criticism and modification, one of them reacted by saying, "This design is great! But why in the world do you call it ideal? We could bring it about tomorrow if we made up our minds to do so."

This stakeholder had responded to what is probably the most important property of an idealized design: It reveals that the *principal obstruction between us and the future we most desire is ourselves.* People consistently project their self-imposed constraints onto the environment, thus absolving themselves of responsibility for their lot. To be sure, the environment does impose constraints on us, but not nearly as many as we impose on ourselves. What we lack most is the will to make the changes that will bring us closer to our hearts' desires. The more satisfied we are with what we have, the less inclined we are to make even short-run sacrifices for long-run gains, particularly when the short-run sacrifices are well defined and the long-run gains are not. Idealized design is a way of defining the potential long-run gains and revealing how much shorter the run can be than we might initially think.

Now we shall present an abbreviated version of an idealized design of a participative democracy. Then we shall consider ways of realizing as much of it as we currently can and of making further progress toward it in the future.

Ideally, such a design should be prepared by all people who hold a stake in it. It was not within our power to seek out such participation, but we did involve as many people as we could. However, this does not justify our imposing the design on others. We present it only in the hope that it will stimulate extensive discussion that will eventually produce a design supported by national consensus.

An Idealized Design of a Participative Democracy

A participative democracy would have a government with no top or bottom, no unidirectional flow of authority from higher to lower. Its government would be characterized by two-directional flows back and forth. It would emphasize responsibility rather than authority and service rather than command. Therefore, we represent such an organization as having lateral rather than vertical relationships (see Figure 2).

Figure 2. A Participative Democracy

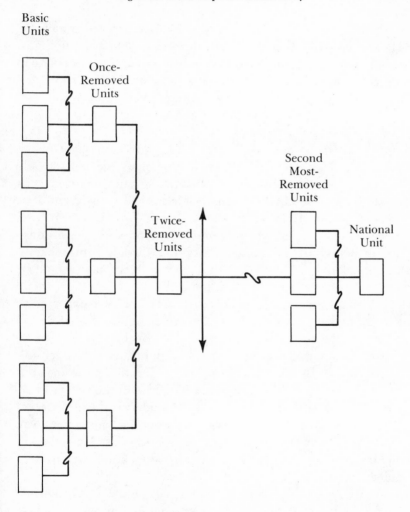

In a participative democracy, the governed would be self-governing to the extent they wanted, and they would have direct control over any other government they created. They would be the ultimate source of the power and resources available for collective use.

The basic unit of government would be small enough to be governed by all its adult members—a committee of the whole, an assembly that reaches decisions by consensus. Therefore, the basic units should contain no more than about 100 adults, for example, a city block or a small village.

What about an area in which there are no residences? Those who work there would be members of the basic unit governing that area. This means that individuals could participate in the governance of more than one basic unit. For instance, people with several homes, each in a different basic unit, would participate in their respective units and the larger units of which each of these is a constituent.

Each basic unit would elect a leader from among its members. The leaders of about ten contiguous basic units would form the next unit of government. These once-removed units would be accountable and responsible to their constituent basic units. Leaders of the once-removed units would in turn form twice-removed units, which would be accountable and responsible to their constituent units. This process would continue until a national unit is formed. The leader of every unit would be elected by the members of that unit.

The leader of every derivative unit would be expected to participate in meetings of its constituent units. Therefore, all leaders of derivative units except the national leader would participate in their respective constituent units and the larger unit of which each of these is a constituent. Then all unit leaders but those of the basic and once-removed units and the two most removed would interact directly with leaders of five different units: two more removed, two less removed, and their own. Such interaction would facilitate their tasks of (vertically) coordinating and (horizontally) integrating the actions of different units.

If basic units contain about 100 adults, and once-removed units are formed by bringing about ten basic units together, and so on, the number of people represented by each unit of the resulting society would be somewhat as follows:

Unit Degree of Removal	Adult Population Represented
0	100
1	1,000
2	10,000
3	100,000
4	1,000,000
5	10,000,000
6	100,000,000

These numbers are not fixed. Several considerations would affect the actual number and size of units. For example, if states or cities are retained as political units, as they might well be, different ones would have different numbers of units. If, for example, fifty states were retained in the design, the leaders of these states could constitute a national assembly, congress, or parliament. One or two members of each state unit could also serve in a second house of congress. Many other variations are possible.

Basic units could do whatever they wanted provided that their actions had no effect on any other basic unit. Any actions that could affect other basic units would require the approval of the units affected or, if they did not approve, of the closest unit of government responsible to all the basic units affected. Derivative units would be able to do anything they are empowered to do by their constituent units as long as their actions did not affect units outside their jurisdictions or other units at the same level. All power would flow from the basic units; all responsibility would flow to them.

All money accumulated by any level of government in excess of its budgeted operating costs would be allocated on a per capita basis to the basic units to which it is responsible unless the basic units decide otherwise. In 1980, for example, all expenditures by governments in the United States, excluding those for defense, amounted to about $3,000 per capita. If only half of this had been allocated to a basic unit containing 100 adults and 50 children, that unit would have received $225,000 for the year!

Budgets of all derivative units would require approval by

their constituent units. Units could pool their resources to provide or obtain jointly desired services or facilities, such as trash collection, road maintenance, or police and fire protection. No unit of government would be able to levy taxes on less-removed units or individuals without their approval. Any unit could derive income from the provision of services if the conditions set forth in Chapter Five are met.

The national government in this participative democracy would have only those powers given to it by less-removed units of government. It would be likely to receive such powers when economies of scale applied or where there was a need for centralized coordination and control, for example, in defense, immigration, and aviation control. Whatever could be better done at a unit closer to the people would be.

No one would be compelled to participate in the governance of his or her basic unit. Participation would be voluntary, but anyone who did not participate would nevertheless be bound by the collective decisions made.

This design of a participative democracy should not be confused with either the so-called New Federalism supported by President Reagan or Jacksonian democracy. In both of these, the federal government delegates power to units subordinate to it: "The Reaganite shift of programs to states [is] 'the transfer of pseudopower' for without resources not much can be achieved. To empower people should not be mainly a policy of less resources but one of more choices in the ways that resources can be used" (Miller and Tomaskovic-Devey, 1983, p. 154).

This idea is correct, but it misses the main point. In our current system, even if resources are moved down to lower-level units of government along with authority and responsibility, these units depend on a level of government *further* removed from the governed. The allocation of resources from the top *down* is what made corruption so prevalent in Jacksonian democracy. Government officials who are responsible to others further removed from the governed than they are are much more tempted to engage in corruption than those responsible to people who are closer to the governed. Basic units in a participative democracy can be expected to monitor closely the use of the resources that they ultimately control. Derivative units can also be expected to monitor closely the use of the resources that they have allocated to more-removed units.

Participative democracy is currently approximated in some neighborhood associations, cooperatives, professional societies, and trade associations. In trade associations, for example, corporate members are the source of funds, and each is normally represented on the governing board. The association has no power over its members; it is their servant, doing only what it is asked to do. In brief, it serves the common interests of the members without reducing their autonomy. Members are free to leave the association for another whenever they so desire.

It should be apparent that the participative democracy described here would demonopolize and debureaucratize government. This would make the adoption of the measures proposed in this book more probable. In addition, because smaller units of government would have the ability and resources to acquire or provide services, demand for them would be likely to increase significantly. All this, we believe, would increase employment considerably.

Moreover, since ultimate responsibility for unemployment would rest with the basic units, they and other units of government close to them would be likely to find or create useful employment for the unemployed. At the very least, one would expect the unemployed to do such things as improve and maintain the local environment and public buildings, assist in daycare centers and schools, create and operate recreational facilities, and assist the elderly and disabled. In rural areas they might work unused farms and engage in such activities as the Civilian Conservation Corps did a number of years ago.

Toward an Idealized Participative Democracy

The Spanish philosopher Jose Ortega y Gasset (1966, p. 1) wrote:

> Man has been able to grow enthusiastic over his vision of . . . unconvincing enterprises. He has put himself to work for the sake of an idea, seeking

by magnificent exertions to arrive at the incredible. And in the end, he has arrived there. Beyond all doubt it is one of the vital sources of man's power, to be thus able to kindle enthusiasm from the mere glimmer of something improbable, difficult, remote.

The public has been activated in the names of many causes that captured its imagination and channeled its (often latent) desires. But can the idea of a participative democracy by itself mobilize people to participate in a social movement directed at its realization? Citizen groups in communities across the country have increasingly been taking affairs into their own hands. Peter Johnson (1984, p. 1) cited the following communities, among others, as receiving the All-America Cities Award for successful citizen action programs:

> Ardmore, Oklahoma, where $3 million worth of road work comes from a citizen-supported sales tax.
> Cleveland, where citizens set up shelters for homeless, a neighborhood program to keep homeowners from moving, and a job program for youths.
> St. Paul, Minnesota, where citizens helped develop an "energy efficient" heating system for a housing project.
> Tacoma, Washington, where residents set up programs for the disabled and unemployed.

Richard Louv (1984) points out a social development of even greater relevance:

> In a single decade, a whole new level of democratic self-rule has arisen: tens of thousands of private minigovernments, called community associations, are controlling common-interest communities. For the first time, local government faces a private government competitor in the delivery of public service. . . .
> The range of goods and services bought by these associations is impressive. Fancy electronic surveillance systems, telephone-answering services,

private police, central utilities, and homeowners insurance are all purchased with the leverage of group buying power. . . . As a result, the cost of such coverage is often reduced by as much as 60 percent. Some community associations are even buying group vacations and communal computers [pp. 130, 133].

The public appears to be ripe for mobilization. It has been viewing with increasing alarm the rapidly rising cost and power of government, the loss by individuals of self-determination and self-sufficiency, and the abuse of consumers by public and private providers of goods and services.

The cost of government has increased dramatically since 1929. Its purchases of goods and services increased from 8.8 percent of the GNP in 1929 to 20.3 percent in 1981. The public has been reacting to this. For example, through the passage of Proposition 13 the people of California limited the expenditures of the state's government. Such revolt is also reflected in numerous local rejections of proposals to increase expenditures on such public services as police, fire protection, and education. Despite continuously increasing expenditures on education, many people feel that its quality has deteriorated significantly. The same is true of urban infrastructures. In addition, stories of wasteful spending by big government, particularly in defense, have become commonplace.

There is also a growing sense of powerlessness among people who depend on government for essential services and the condition of their environment. They find government service agencies unresponsive and often abusive. The governed resent being treated like undeserving subjects or supplicants. It is not that they want more care and attention from government—they want to be less dependent on it. They want to control more of their own lives. Americans and their primary communities have long greatly valued self-determination and self-sufficiency. Americans prefer to live in predominantly self-service communities.

There is an increasing number of examples in which small communities with participative governments provide themselves with better services at a lower cost than big governments provide. For example, Fernando Solana, former secretary of education in Mexico, turned federal funds over to small villages so that they could provide their own educational services. The funds had to be administered democratically by the community. The result was education at least as good as that provided by federally operated schools at only a fraction of the cost. Moreover, this program brought education to thousands of small communities for the first time.

The growing consumerist movement in a number of MDCs, particularly in the United States, might well be redirected to focus on services rather than goods. The average consumer is spending more on services than on goods, but consumer advocates continue to focus on products.

To the extent that these three issues—expensive government, expansive government, and abuse of service consumers—can be brought into sharp focus, public pressure can be built *against* hierarchically structured, bureaucratic, monopolistic government and *for* participative democracy.

Unfortunately, it is easier to mobilize the public into an effort either to protect something it has or to rid itself of something it has but does not want than it is to mobilize it in an effort to obtain something it wants but does not have. Barbara Ward (1968, p. 75) asked: "Is imagination liberated only when destruction is at issue? Are we to be aroused by our fears and hates and never by our loves?" Even the American Revolution was directed more against abusive English rule than toward national autonomy. If England's rule had not been so oppressive, it is doubtful that the Revolution would have occurred.

Nevertheless, there have been major social movements motivated by love rather than hate. Certainly the rise of Christianity is a case in point, even if subsequent sectarian divisions are not. In most cases, however, social movements have had both a push and a pull. Women's liberation and the civil rights movement, for example, are both pushed by discrimination and pulled by a desire for equality.

It is difficult to mobilize people against abuses by governments under which they enjoy a relatively high standard of living and quality of life, particularly if they believe both will improve further. It will take a very strong pull to mobilize them to transform their societies so that they can revitalize their economies. Can the concept of a participative democracy provide this pull?

One thing is clear: The economies of the West will not be revitalized until their democracies are.

10

Conclusion: Revitalizing Western Economies

Productive employment is the most effective and satisfactory way that societies have yet found for simultaneously producing and distributing wealth. Therefore, a high rate of unemployment is a measure of an economy's lack of vitality. To the extent that a society does not provide productive employment to all who desire it, it is seriously deficient no matter how much growth it exhibits as measured by other criteria.

We have argued that even with economic recovery, prospects are not very good for significantly reducing the current high rates of unemployment in Western MDCs. These countries are coming down from the crest of employment generated by production industries—mining, construction, and manufacturing. The percentages of their labor forces employed in these industries are decreasing and are likely to continue to do so for the following reasons:

1. labor-intensive industries in MDCs will continue to migrate to LDCs, where less expensive and sufficiently skilled labor is abundant;
2. those production industries that remain in MDCs will have to increase their mechanization and automation in order to maintain their competitiveness in the international marketplace; and

3. the increase in the demand for goods in MDCs has slowed and is likely to continue doing so.

This does not mean that the production of goods in MDCs will decrease, but it does imply that a decreasing percentage of the labor force will be engaged in such production. A similar development took place in agriculture as a result of its mechanization and industrialization.

Meanwhile, the work forces in MDCs will grow because:

1. their populations will increase despite declining birth rates,
2. an increasing percentage of women are likely to enter the work force, and
3. absenteeism and retirement are likely to decrease because of declining morbidity and increasing life expectancy brought about by advances in medicine.

These trends will increase unemployment unless there is a significant change in Western societies and their institutions, particularly their governments and corporations.

We have also shown that governments of MDCs have not been intervening in their economies in ways that significantly reduce unemployment. Their interventions have been directed at:

1. alleviating the poverty resulting from unemployment,
2. reducing the work force by encouraging emigration and discouraging immigration,
3. training people for and moving them to jobs that are unfilled or expected,
4. protecting existing jobs, and
5. creating new jobs.

However humanitarian and politically expedient the first four of these interventions may be, *they do not create jobs*. Some of them redistribute wealth more equitably, but they do so at a high cost to society, thereby reducing the amount of wealth available for distribution.

On the other hand, the efforts of government to create

new jobs have not been effective. These include: (1) increasing public employment, (2) providing incentives intended to create more private employment, (3) work sharing, and (4) inducing employers to locate within a government's jurisdiction.

Jobs created in the public sector too often consist of make-work. Such work does not produce wealth; it consumes wealth. This induces inflation, and inflation reduces the standard of living.

Publicly subsidized private employment is generally short-lived because, even with financial support from government, additional jobs can seldom be justified when there is a lack of demand for their output. If there is such a demand, subsidies are not required.

Work sharing divides a fixed amount of work among more people; it creates more jobs, but not more work. It usually increases an employer's costs substantially because the employed are not willing to accept sufficiently reduced compensation.

Finally, enticing employers to locate their facilities where a government wants them to does not create new jobs; it only moves them.

As a result of the ineffectiveness of governmental efforts, a number of proposals have been made for revitalizing economies. These have been of four major types: (1) dialogue, (2) industrial policy, (3) socioeconomic reform, and (4) a radical transformation of society.

Dialogues between representatives of different economic sectors have seldom produced suggestions that governments have followed; those few that have been followed have not been effective. We see no reason to believe that dialogues will be more effective in the future than they have been in the past. Because these representatives normally try to protect their own interests, their dialogues seldom produce substantive proposals.

Industrial policy recommendations are generally directed at reindustrialization, the revitalization of production industries. As we pointed out, this is unlikely to increase employment significantly; in fact, it is likelier to reduce it. The industrial policies that are proposed tend to focus on revitalizing large and often less efficient industries that many people believe are better left to struggle for economic survival. Most new jobs in industry are being created by small companies, many of which have short lives or little growth. None of the proposed policies provide an effective way of selecting those small companies that will survive and grow.

Some people believe that the changes required to revitalize our economies cannot be implemented without political reforms. Lester Thurow (1981) is prominent among them. He argues that we need a consistent set of industrial policies directed at economic equity, which in turn requires a parliamentary system of government. But he fails to explain why parliamentary governments in Europe have been even less successful than the U.S. government in revitalizing their economies. He also proposes massive employment by government to solve the unemployment problem but specifies that such employment be productive. However, he does not reveal how this can be assured.

Finally, people such as Hazel Henderson (1978) argue for radical social change. She advocates pushing government down to small primary communities and replacing economic growth with improved quality of life as a societal objective. She argues that only through networks of small, self-governing units can our economic problems be solved without degrading our environment. She also proposes a number of interventions for the central government, including resource conservation programs, policies to foster the conversion to low-capital-investment and labor-intensive industries, and strong antitrust measures. But she does not deal with the apparent contradiction between stronger centralized control and decentralized communal self-government. Nor does she bring her numerous proposals together into a cohesive, consistent redesign of society.

We accept the need for dialogue among an economy's stakeholders, but we believe it will be ineffectual unless these people can implement their decisions. Furthermore, we believe that *all* people who hold a stake in the outcome of a dialogue—not only their representatives—should have the opportunity to participate. How to bring about an extensive national dialogue is a matter requiring social design. We have proposed such a design.

We agree with advocates of industrial policy that obstructions to economic development (in contrast to economic growth) should either be removed or circumvented. But we believe that this cannot be done by treating obstructions independently of each other. They must be treated as an interacting set that can only be dealt with effectively by redesigning the political and economic system. Changing the behavior of the existing system is not enough.

We agree with advocates of socioeconomic reform that changes in government are required to bring about economic improvements. But we do not believe that modification of a strong centralized government is the kind of change required. Decentralization of government is required.

Finally, we agree with advocates of radical social change that the changes required are both structural and functional and that these must have the effect of returning government to the people. But we also believe that such changes have little chance of being brought about unless a comprehensive redesign of society is presented. Even with such a design the task is formidable; without it the task is impossible.

The objective of redesigning society should be societal development, not economic growth. A country can develop without growing, and it can grow without developing. Economic growth, an increase in the standard of living, should be sought only to the extent that it is compatible with development. Growth should be treated as a means, not an end.

An individual or a group develops when it increases its ability and desire to satisfy its own needs and desires and those of others. Development is more a matter of learning than earning. No individual or group can develop another because one cannot learn for another. One can only develop oneself. A government cannot develop the governed, but it can and should encourage and facilitate their development. This suggests that *a government should not try to solve the unemployment problem, but should encourage and facilitate solution of the problem by the governed.*

How can government provide such encouragement and facilitation? To answer this question we must first reexamine and reformulate the unemployment problem.

We have argued that production industries in MDCs are unlikely to generate a large number of new jobs. If jobs are to be created, they must be created in the service sector. The desire for services has been growing continuously as the standard of living has increased. The higher the standard of living, the more attention is given to the quality of life. Quality of life depends critically on the amount, availability, accessibility, and quality of services.

However, much of the growing *desire* for services has not been translated into *demand* because of their high cost, low quality, and offensive manner of delivery. Consequently, many jobs that could be created to provide desired services have not been. However, they can be created by decreasing the cost, increasing the quality, and improving the delivery of services.

The defects in services derive from the fact that most are provided by bureaucratic monopolies either within government or the private sector. Therefore, solving the unemployment problem lies in debureaucratizing and demonopolizing public and private providers of service.

Governments can go a long way toward creating an efficient, consumer-oriented, wealth-producing service sector by:

1. enabling the private sector to compete for the right to provide as many services as possible that are now provided by governments,
2. requiring consumers to pay directly for as many services as possible,
3. subsidizing consumers who cannot pay for necessary services rather than subsidizing suppliers,
4. assuring competitive sources of as many services as possible even when they are provided exclusively by public agencies, and,
5. where a supplier must be subsidized, doing so according to the quantity and quality of services provided.

In addition, governments should initiate participative QWL programs in all public service agencies. The productivity and quality of service work can be significantly increased through such programs. Satisfied service workers who have opportunities for personal development and advancement are inclined to provide high-quality, efficient service.

Such government actions as we have proposed will not by themselves solve the unemployment problem, but they can encourage and facilitate actions by other people who can solve the problem. However, we do not believe governments are likely to take these actions unless considerable public pressure is applied. For this reason, we consider the role of the public in solving the unemployment problem.

Turning to corporations, we consider what they can do to help themselves and to accelerate the transition to a wealth-producing, service-based economy. First, we suggest that corporations diversify into services by:

1. offering services to others that corporations already efficiently provide to themselves,
2. providing services corporations currently obtain from external suppliers but providing them more efficiently and effectively, and
3. providing services that are either required to use their products or that require use of these products.

Second, we propose the development of new or the redevelopment of old products, processes, and facilities that are either: (1) more appropriate for LDCs, (2) required by increasingly automated systems in MDCs, or (3) capable of creating new or improving old services.

Finally, we suggested three ways of increasing corporate productivity: (1) using QWL programs, (2) rationalizing corporate processes, particularly management systems, and (3) collaboration within and between corporations and between corporations, government, unions, and the public.

Corporations are more likely to pursue our proposals than are governments, because our proposals for corporations are compatible with their self-interests; those for government are not. The pressure of competition is often enough to induce corporations to explore new directions. This is not true of governments.

Public officials are not likely to adopt any of our proposals for governments because they would reduce the size, power, and number of government agencies. Many of the officials' jobs would be jeopardized. Therefore, our proposals are not likely to be adopted without a great deal of public pressure. Such pressure should be directed at demonopolizing and debureaucratizing government itself. This requires fundamental changes in the structure and functions of government—returning government *to* the people, converting it to *participative democracy*.

In a participative democracy, small, self-governing units are the source of the authority and responsibility assigned to other units of government, and they determine the use and allotment of resources. The basic units can do whatever they want as long as they do not prevent other units from doing what they want. Actions that adversely affect another unit require that unit's approval. Disagreements that cannot be resolved are settled by the most local unit of government responsible to all the affected units. This principle applies to all types of units.

Representatives of the basic units form once-removed units of government. Representatives of these units in turn form twice-removed units and so on, up to the national government. All representatives are elected by their entire constituencies. Starting with basic units, each unit of government monitors the actions of the closest aggregated unit of which it is part. Services can be provided or procured by basic units or, with approval of these units, by more removed units. Even when provided by more removed units, these services would be monitored by the basic units affected.

Conversion to a participative democracy would, we believe, demonopolize and debureaucratize government as well as public and private providers of services. This, in turn, would decrease the cost and increase the quality of services and improve their delivery, enabling demand for them to grow. As a result, a large number of jobs would be created that would significantly reduce, if not eliminate, the unemployment problem.

The transformation of our society to a participative democracy is compatible with a growing trend toward self-government and self-sufficiency in small communities. However, it will not be easy to start up independent initiatives and develop them into a national movement to make such a transformation. Satisfaction with the status quo is too widespread among people not directly affected by such problems as unemployment and high-cost, low-quality services. It remains to be seen whether the concept of a participative democracy can be presented so as to mobilize the public. Such a presentation requires inspiring leadership. It also remains to be seen whether the concept of participative democracy, the desire to solve the unemployment problem, and the desire for national development can give rise to such leadership.

The changes we advocate are not imminent, and they are not likely to occur spontaneously. If they occur at all, it will be in an evolutionary, not a revolutionary, way. The rate of their evolution will depend on the state of our economies. Futurists expect our economies to fluctuate increasingly, to experience shorter periods of prosperity and more frequent and more severe recessions and depressions. Should the magnitude and frequency of such economic contractions increase as expected, the public may become mobilized to change the structure of the government in the near future.

In the meantime, persistently high rates of unemployment will create new social problems and exacerbate old ones. Unemployment will become increasingly costly to the employed and disrupt their "good life." It will nibble at the fabric of our societies and the consciences of those who believe everyone has a right to live above the poverty level with a satisfying quality of life.

Our proposals are only suggestions, not prescriptions, designed to stimulate the search for and exploration of new ideas. The old ideas, however they may be repackaged, are not revitalizing our economies, improving our quality of life, or accelerating national development. We must design the future we want and invent ways of approximating that future as closely as possible.

References

"A&P Looks Like Tengelmann's Vietnam." *Business Week,* February 1, 1982, pp. 42-44.

Ackoff, R. L. *Redesigning the Future.* New York: Wiley, 1974.

Ackoff, R. L. *Creating the Corporate Future.* New York: Wiley, 1981.

Ackoff, R. L., and others. *Designing a National Scientific and Technological Communication System: The SCATT Report.* Philadelphia: University of Pennsylvania Press, 1976.

Arenson, K. W. "Epidemic of Recession Poses Hard Choices for All Nations." *The New York Times,* November 5, 1982, p. A1.

Bartlett, B. R. "Industrial Policy Crisis for Liberal Economists." *Fortune,* November 14, 1983, pp. 83-86.

Birch, D. "Who Creates Jobs?" *The Public Interest,* Fall 1981, pp. 3-14.

Bureau of the Census, U.S. Department of Commerce. *Statis-*

tical Abstract of the United States. Washington, D.C.: U.S. Government Printing Office, 1978.

Bureau of the Census, U.S. Department of Commerce. *Social Indicators III.* Washington, D.C.: U.S. Government Printing Office, 1980a.

Bureau of the Census, U.S. Department of Commerce. *World Population 1979.* Washington, D.C.: U.S. Government Printing Office, 1980b.

Bureau of the Census, U.S. Department of Commerce. *Statistical Abstract of the United States.* Washington, D.C.: U.S. Government Printing Office, 1981.

Bureau of the Census, U.S. Department of Commerce. *Statistical Abstract of the United States.* Washington, D.C.: U.S. Government Printing Office, 1982.

Cars for Cities. Report of the Steering Group and Working Group Appointed by the Ministry of Transport. London: H.M. Stationery Office, 1967.

Contini, B. "The Second Economy of Italy." In V. Tanzi (Ed.), *The Underground Economy in the United States and Abroad.* Lexington: Lexington Books, 1982.

Dockins, B. "Trust and Cooperation, We Can Make It Work." *309 Review,* January 1983.

Eizenstat, S. E. "Not If, But How." *Fortune,* January 23, 1984, pp. 183-185.

Eldred, J. C. "Labor Management Committee Improves the Quality of Working Life." *New Directions for Education and Work,* 1978, *3,* 81-87.

Emery, F. E., and Thorsrud, E. *Form and Content in Industrial Democracy.* London: Tavistock, 1969.

Employee Assistance Programs: A Model. Washington, D.C.: U.S. Brewers Association, 1981.

"Funny Money and the Poor." *The New York Times,* February 25, 1983, p. A30.

Gans, H. "Jobs and Services: Toward a Labor-Intensive Economy." (Reprint.) New York: Center for Policy Research, September 1976.

Gans, H. J. "Jobs and Services: Toward a Labor-Intensive Economy." *Challenge,* July/August 1977, pp. 41-45.

"Gyllenhammar's Vigilantes." *The Economist*, January 28, 1984, p. 67.

Hanke, S. H. "Privately Providing Public Services." *The New York Times*, March 29, 1984, p. A27.

Henderson, B. D. *Inflation: A Systems Hypothesis*. Boston: The Boston Consulting Group, 1982.

Henderson, H. *Creating Alternative Futures: The End of Economics*. New York: Berkley Windover Books, 1978.

"How Democrats Might Recapture the Growth Issue." *Business Week*, November 28, 1983, p. 28.

"Interview with Anne Rice." *Self*, February 1983, p. 69.

Irons, D. "Inching Toward a National Competitive Strategy." *Harvard Magazine*, November-December 1983, pp. 44-49.

Jencks, C. "Giving Parents Money for Schooling: Education Vouchers." *Phi Delta Kappan*, September 1970, pp. 49-52.

Jenkins, D. "QWL—Current Trends and Directions." Occasional Paper No. 3. Ontario Quality of Working Life Centre, Ontario Ministry of Labour, Toronto, December 1981.

Johnson, P. "All-American Honors for Working Together." *USA Today*, April 9, 1984, p. 1.

Jun, N. "Another Development for Japan." *International Foundation for Development Alternatives Dossier*, 1980, *15*, 47-62.

Kennedy, J. L. "Industrial Revitalization Will Add Few Engineering Jobs." *The Philadelphia Inquirer*, February 26, 1984, p. L1.

Lasch, C. "The Degradation of Work and the Apotheosis of Art." *Harper's*, February 1984, pp. 40-45.

Louv, R. "Control Thy Neighbor." *Review*, April 1984, pp. 129-140.

Magaziner, I. C., and Reich, R. B. *Minding America's Business*. New York: Harcourt Brace Jovanovich, 1982.

Mansfield, E. *Industrial Research and Technological Innovation*. New York: Norton, 1968.

Meadows, D. H., and others. *The Limits to Growth*. New York: Signet, 1972.

Merritt, G. "The Job Gap." *World Press Review*, December 1982, pp. 37-38.

Miller, S. M., and Tomaskovic-Devey, D. *Recapitalizing America: Alternatives to the Corporate Distortion of National Policy.* Boston: Routledge & Kegan Paul, 1983.

Minicar Transit System. Final Report of Phase 1, Feasibility Study. Prepared by the University of Pennsylvania for the U.S. Department of Transportation, 1968.

Morison, E. B. *Men, Machines and Modern Times.* Cambridge, Mass.: MIT Press, 1966.

Muller, R. E. *Revitalizing America: Politics for Prosperity.* New York: Touchstone Books, 1980.

Naisbitt, J. *Megatrends: Ten New Directions Transforming Our Lives.* New York: Warner Books, 1982.

National Commission on Excellence in Education. "A Nation at Risk: The Imperative for Educational Reform." *The Chronicle of Higher Education,* May 4, 1983, pp. 11–16.

Niskanen, W. A., Jr. *Bureaucracy and Representative Government.* Hawthorne, N.Y.: Aldine, 1971.

Ortega y Gasset, J. *Mission of the University.* New York: Norton, 1966.

Ozbekhan, H. "The Future of Paris: A Systems Study in Strategic Urban Planning." *Philosophical Transactions of the Royal Society London,* 1977, *A287,* 523-544.

Quality of Work Life. Handbook prepared and distributed by United Food and Commercial Workers Local 56 and Local 1357 with Super Fresh Food Markets. Philadelphia, 1983.

Rangachari, K. "The Protectionist Timebomb." *World Press Review,* December 1982, p. 42.

Sagasti, F., and Ackoff, R. L. "Possible and Likely Futures of Urban Transportation." *Socio-Economic Planning,* 1971, *5,* 413-428.

Savas, E. S. *Privatizing the Public Sector: How to Shrink Government.* Chatham, N.J.: Chatham House Publishers, 1982.

Schon, D. A. *Beyond the Stable State.* New York: Random House, 1971.

Schrage, M. "IBM May Enter Software Fray." *The Washington Post,* January 18, 1984, p. F1.

Stein, H. "Don't Fall for Industrial Policy." *Fortune,* November 14, 1983, pp. 64-78.

Stephens, M. D. "On Sinai, There's No Economics." *The New York Times,* November 13, 1981, p. A35.

Tanzi, V. (Ed.). *The Underground Economy in the United States and Abroad.* Lexington: Lexington Books, 1982.

Thurow, L. *The Zero-Sum Society: Distribution and the Possibilities for Economic Change.* New York: Penguin Books, 1981.

Trist, E. "The Evolution of Socio-Technical Systems." Occasional Paper No. 2. Ontario Quality of Working Life Centre, Ontario Ministry of Labour, Toronto, June 1981.

Vinocur, J. "Economic Rigidity Hampers Western Europe." *The New York Times,* December 1, 1982, p. A1.

Ward, B. *The Lopsided World.* New York: Norton, 1968.

Weber, M. *Economy and Society.* (J. C. B. Mohr, Trans.) Berkeley: University of California Press, 1978.

West, R. R., and Logue, D. E. "The False Doctrines of Productivity." *The New York Times,* January 9, 1983, p. F3.

"Worker Ownership May Save Some A&Ps." *Business Week,* June 28, 1982, pp. 44-45.

"World Economy Survey." *The Economist,* September 24, 1983, p. 17.

"Would Industrial Policy Help Small Business?" *Business Week,* February 6, 1984, p. 72.

Index